Cycling in
Wales

Fergal MacErlean

Editor: Donna Wood
Designer: Phil Barfoot
Copy Editor: Helen Ridge
Proofreader: Judith Forshaw
Picture Researchers: Lesley Grayson (AA)
and Jonathan Bewley (Sustrans)
Image retouching and internal repro:
Sarah Montgomery and James Tims
Cartography provided by the Mapping Services
Department of AA Publishing from data supplied by
Richard Sanders and Sustrans mapping team
Research and development by: Lindsey Ryle, Melissa
Henry, Julian Hunt and Sustrans regional staff
Supplementary text: Nick Cotton
Production: Lorraine Taylor

Produced by AA Publishing

ISBN: 978-0-7495-7254-9

Published by AA Publishing (a trading name of
AA Media Limited, whose registered office is
Fanum House, Basing View, Basingstoke
RG21 4EA; registered number 06112600).

A04632

Free cycling permits are required on some British
Waterways canal towpaths. Visit www.waterscape.com
or call 0845 671 5530.

The National Cycle Network has been made possible
by the support and co-operation of hundreds of
organisations and thousands of individuals, including:
local authorities and councils, central governments
and their agencies, the National Lottery, landowners,
utility and statutory bodies, countryside and
regeneration bodies, the Landfill Communities Fund,
other voluntary organisations, charitable trusts and
foundations, the cycle trade and industry, corporate
sponsors, community organisations and Sustrans'
supporters. Sustrans would also like to extend thanks
to the thousands of volunteers who generously
contribute their time to looking after their local
sections of the Network.

We have taken all reasonable steps to ensure that
the cycle rides in this book are safe and achievable
by people with a reasonable level of fitness. However,
all outdoor activities involve a degree of risk and the
publishers accept no responsibility for any injuries
caused to readers while following these cycle rides.

The contents of this book are believed correct at the
time of printing. Nevertheless, the publishers cannot
be held responsible for any errors or omissions or for
changes in the details given in this book or for the
consequences of any reliance on the information
provided by the same. This does not affect your
statutory rights.

Printed and bound in Dubai by Oriental Press
theAA.com/shop

Sustrans
2 Cathedral Square
College Green
Bristol BS1 5DD
www.sustrans.org.uk

Sustrans is a Registered Charity in the UK:
Number 326550 (England and Wales)
SCO39263 (Scotland).

CONTENTS

THE RIDES

Bikes have been m
of transport since

Foreword by **Miranda Krestovnikoff,** zoologist and broadcaster

Cycling for me is all about making the most of your free time to get closer to the world around you.

Picturing my favourite bike ride, I'd be on a quiet, coastal lane with a gentle sea breeze at my back. The winding road would head steadily uphill, where the reward at the top would be a charming country pub, beyond which would hopefully be a long, freewheeling descent to ease off a well-earned lunch.

This is how I always imagine being in Pembrokeshire. I've spent many a blissful hour here on the Celtic Trail as it winds up and down through Fishguard and around the coast at St David's towards Tenby. The scenery here is varied and wonderful: from sandy coves to rich, green hills dotted with lazily grazing sheep.

But this is just one picture of Wales. Further along the Celtic Trail are the gravel trails and traffic-free paths through Pembrey Forest and the Millennium Coastal Park – arguably the best example we have in Britain of post-industrial regeneration.

Then there are the regenerated canals and railway lines of the Valleys, which make for a glorious family-friendly ride and epitomize how our industrial heritage is a recurring theme throughout Wales's 1,200 miles (1,930km) of National Cycle Network. Further north, the Lôn Las Ogwen ascends through former railway tracks and an old slate quarry for panoramic views of Snowdonia.

"Cycling for me is all about making the most of your free time to get closer to the world around you."

Bikes have been my main form of transport since childhood. In fact, I have never owned a car and I'm comfortable (and fit!) enough to not think twice about pedalling into Wales from my home in the West Country. But another of the Network's strong points is that it gives novice cyclists the confidence to get back on their bikes. So I've ridden with my husband through the Wye Valley, which includes the Peregrine Path – an easily achievable six-mile jaunt through some of the UK's finest scenery. I hope to be taking my two young children on this route soon and give them the cycling bug!

And cycling is about more than the view around the next corner because you become immersed in your ever-changing surroundings. So on one single ride you could have an unexpected chill from the early morning mist, the warmth from the sun shining through the overhanging trees and – let's be honest – an absolute soaking from the North Atlantic drift!

There are many more routes that await me and, looking through this guide, I hope you'll feel the same buzz of anticipation for broadening your experiences of this wonderfully diverse country.

View towards the Black Mountains

Taking a breather at Burry Port

> "Cycling is about more than the view around the next corner..."

Precipice Walk, Snowdonia National Park

Miranda is a zoologist and television presenter and regularly presents natural history items on BBC2's Coast and BBC1's The One Show. She has been a Sustrans supporter for over five years.

INTRODUCTION

Unless you happen to have a friendly dragon at your disposal, there can be no more magical way to travel through Wales than by bicycle. The compact nature of the country is ideally suited to exploration on two wheels. This ancient landscape is a place of exceptional natural beauty, with eye-catching lakes, dramatic mountains and a spectacular coastline.

Caernarfon Castle

Sustrans Cymru welcomes you to the 1,200 miles (1,930km) of National Cycle Network in Wales. The Network extends the length and breadth of the country, with lots of traffic-free and quiet road sections, ideal for family cycling. This guide highlights a selection of these, all of which make a superb day out. And, for the most part, there aren't too many hills.

The National Routes in Wales, in common with those in the rest of the UK, allow you to explore on well-surfaced and signed cycleways. The main ones detailed in this guide are sections of these longer-distance rides: the North Wales Coast Cycle Route (Route 5), from Anglesey to Chester; the Taff Trail (Route 8), from Brecon to Cardiff; Lôn Cambria (Route 81), from Aberystwyth to Shrewsbury; Lôn Teifi (Route 82), from Aberystwyth to Fishguard; and

the Celtic Trail (Routes 4 and 47), which follows the south coast from Chepstow to Fishguard.

As you follow the routes in this guide, you'll discover that Wales is full of country lanes, old railway lines and canal towpaths, which are quiet, safe and perfect for cycling. Along the way, you'll become immersed in the rich history, both medieval and modern, of this proud nation. Wales has around 600 castles, and routes in this guide pass by several impressive fortresses, such as Monmouth Castle, birthplace of Henry V.

Wales can also boast no fewer than three National Parks: Snowdonia in the north, with its rocky, majestic mountains and long coastline; the Brecon Beacons in the south, where there are lush river valleys and gently rounded hills; and, in the extreme southwest, the

Easy traffic-free cycling

Sebastian Boyesen's 'Guardian' sculpture

Sgwd yr Eira Waterfall

Pembrokeshire coast, with its important wildlife habitats.

The Network passes through all of these magnificent areas. One ride detailed in this guide takes you beneath the rocky giants of Snowdonia, and it also passes the world's largest slate quarry – a potent reminder of the country's legacy of mining and industry. It is impossible to overstate the role that Wales played in the birth of the Industrial Revolution. In particular, the Valleys of south Wales changed the face of the world – coal, hewn by hand from the numerous mines, powered the iron furnaces, bringing great prosperity to their owners. By 1830, Monmouthshire and East Glamorgan were producing half the iron exported by Britain. The Valleys town of Blaenavon, declared a World Heritage Site in 2000, had it all – influential ironworks and a coal mine, now the National Coal Museum. Many of these historic sites can be reached on the ever-expanding National Cycle Network via the old canals and railways that once hauled iron, silver, tin and slate to the ports.

There's never been a better time to cycle in Wales but, before you go, here are a few Welsh words and phrases to help you along the way:

Lôn – Lane
Llyn – Lake
Afon – River
Cwm – Valley
Bore da – Good morning
Sut mae? – How are you?
Peint i fi! – Mine's a pint!
Dwi bron â llwgi allen i fwyta fel ceffyl! – I'm so hungry I could eat a horse!

NATIONAL CYCLE NETWORK FACTS & FIGURES

Most of the routes featured here are part of the National Cycle Network. The aim of this book is to enable you to sample some of the highlights of the region on two wheels, but the rides given here are really just a taster, as there are more than 13,000 miles of Network throughout the UK to explore. More than three-quarters of us live within two miles of one of the routes.

Over one million journeys a day are made on the National Cycle Network; for special trips like fun days out and holiday bike rides, but also the necessary everyday trips; taking people to school, to work, to the shops, to visit each other and to seek out green spaces. Half of these journeys are made on foot and half by bike, with urban traffic-free sections of the Network seeing the most usage.

The National Cycle Network is host to one of the UK's biggest collections of public art. Sculptures, benches, water fountains, viewing points and award-winning bridges enhance its pathways, making Sustrans one of the most prolific commissioners of public art in the UK.

The Network came into being following the award of the first-ever grant from the lottery, through the Millennium Commission, in 1995. Funding for the Network also came from bike retailers and manufacturers through the Bike Hub, as well as local authorities and councils UK-wide, and Sustrans' many supporters. Over 2,500 volunteer Rangers give their time to Sustrans to assist in the maintenance of the National Cycle Network by adopting sections of route in communities throughout the UK. They remove glass and litter, cut back vegetation and try to ensure routes are well signed.

Developing and maintaining the National Cycle Network is just one of the ways in which Sustrans pursues its vision of a world in which people can choose to travel in ways that benefit their health and the environment.

We hope that you enjoy using this book to explore the paths and cycleways of the National Cycle Network and we would like to thank the many hundreds of organisations who have worked with Sustrans to develop the walking and cycling routes, including every local authority and council in the UK.

MAP LEGEND

– – – – – – –	◯	▬ ▬ ▬ ▬ ▬ ▬
Traffic Free/On Road route	Ride Start or Finish Point	National Cycle Network (Traffic Free)

National Cycle Network (On Road)

PH	AA recommended pub		Farm or animal centre		Theme park
	Abbey, cathedral or priory		Garden	*i*	Tourist Information Centre
	Abbey, cathedral or priory in ruins		Hill-fort		Viewpoint
	Aquarium		Historic house		Visitor or heritage centre
	Aqueduct or viaduct		Industrial attraction	◉	World Heritage Site (UNESCO)
	Arboretum		Marina		Zoo or wildlife collection
✕	Battle site		Monument		AA golf course
	Bird Reserve (RSPB)		Museum or gallery		Stadium
	Cadw (Welsh Heritage) site		National Nature Reserve:		Indoor Arena
▲	Campsite		England, Scotland, Wales		Tennis
	Caravan site		Local nature reserve		Horse racing
	Caravan & campsite		National Trust property		Rugby Union
	Castle		National Trust for Scotland property		Football
	Cave		Picnic site		Athletics
	Country park		Roman remains		Motorsports
	English Heritage site		Steam railway		County cricket

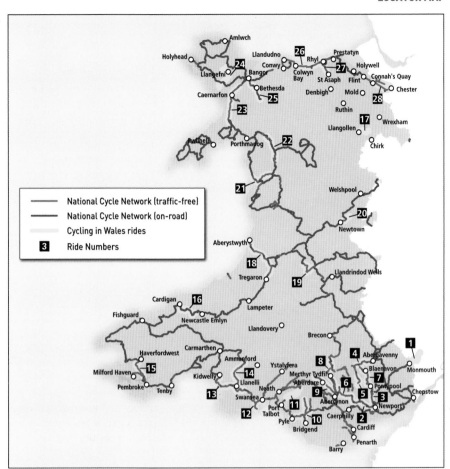

KEY TO LOCATOR MAP

CYCLING WITH CHILDREN

Kids love bikes and love to ride. Cycling helps them to grow up fit, healthy and independent, and introduces them to the wider world and the adventure it holds.

TOP TIPS FOR FAMILY BIKE RIDES:

- Take along snacks, drinks and treats to keep their energy and spirit levels up.
- Don't be too ambitious. It's much better that everyone wants to go out again, than all coming home exhausted, tearful and permanently put off cycling.
- Plan your trip around interesting stops and sights along the way. Don't make journey times any longer than children are happy to sit and play at home.
- Even on a fine day, take extra clothes and waterproofs – just in case. Check that trousers and laces can't get caught in the chain when pedalling along.
- Wrap up toddlers. When a young child is on the back of a bike, they won't be generating heat like the person doing all the pedalling!
- Be careful not to pinch their skin when putting their helmet on. It's easily done and often ends in tears. Just place your forefinger between the clip and the chin.
- Ride in a line with the children in the middle of the adults. If there's only one of you, the adult should be at the rear, keeping an eye on all the children in front. Take special care at road junctions.
- Check that children's bikes are ready to ride. Do the brakes and gears work? Is the saddle the right height? Are the tyres pumped up?
- Carry some sticking plasters and antiseptic wipes – kids are far more likely to fall off and graze arms, hands or knees.
- Take a camera to record the trip – memories are made of this.

TRANSPORTING YOUNG CHILDREN ON TWO WHEELS

It's now easier than ever for you to ride your bike with young children.

- **Child seats:** *6 months to five years (one child)*. Once a baby can support its own head (usually at 6–12 months) they can be carried in a child seat. Seats are fitted mainly to the rear of the bike.
- **Trailers:** babies to five years *(up to two children)*. Young babies can be strapped into their car seat and carried in a trailer, and older children can be strapped in and protected from the wind and rain.
- **Tag-along trailer bikes:** *approx four to nine years*. Tag-alongs (the back half of a child's bike attached to the back of an adult one) allow a child to be towed while they either add some of their own pedal power or just freewheel and enjoy the ride.
- **Tow bar:** *approx four to eight years*. A tow bar converts a standard child's bike to a trailer bike by lifting their front wheel from the ground to prevent them from steering, while enabling them to pedal independently. When you reach a safe place, the tow bar can be detached and the child's bike freed.

TEACHING YOUR CHILD TO RIDE

There are lots of ways for children to develop and gain cycling confidence before they head out on their own.

- **Tricycles or trikes:** available for children from ten months to five years old. They have pedals so kids have all the fun of getting around under their own steam.
- **Balance bikes:** are like normal bikes but without the pedals. This means children learn to balance, steer and gain confidence on two wheels while being able to place their feet firmly and safely on the ground.

- **Training wheels:** stabilisers give support to the rear of the bike and are the easiest way to learn to ride but potentially the slowest.

BUYING THE RIGHT BIKE FOR YOUR CHILD

Every child develops differently and they may be ready to learn to ride between the ages of three and seven. When children do progress to their own bike, emphasising the fun aspect will help them take the tumbles in their stride. Encouragement and praise are important to help them persevere.

Children's bikes generally fall into age categories based on the average size of a child of a specific age. There are no hard and fast rules, as long as your child isn't stretched and can reach the brakes safely and change gear easily. It's important to buy your child a bike that fits them rather than one they can grow into. Ask your local bike shop for advice and take your child along to try out different makes and sizes.

To find a specialist cycle retailer near you visit www.thecyclingexperts.co.uk

HOT TIPS & COOL TRICKS...

WHAT TO WEAR

For most of the rides featured in this book you do not need any special clothing or footwear. Shoes that are suitable for walking are also fine for cycling. Looser-fitting trousers allow your legs to move more freely, while tops with zips let you regulate your temperature. In cold weather, take gloves and a warm hat; it's also a good idea to pack a waterproof. If you are likely to be out at dusk, take a bright reflective top. If you start to cycle regularly, you may want to invest in some specialist equipment for longer rides, especially padded shorts and gloves.

WHAT TO TAKE

For a short ride, the minimum you will need is a pump and a small tool bag with a puncture repair kit, just in case. However, it is worth considering the following: water bottle, spare inner tube, 'multi-tool' (available from cycle shops), lock, money, sunglasses, lightweight waterproof (some pack down as small as a tennis ball), energy bars, map, camera and a spare top in case it cools down or to keep you warm when you stop for refreshments.

HOW TO TAKE IT

Rucksacks are fine for light loads but can make your back hot and sweaty. For heavier loads and for longer or more regular journeys, you are better off with panniers that attach to a bike rack.

BIKE ACCESSORIES

You may also want to invest in a helmet. A helmet will not prevent accidents from happening but can provide protection if you do fall off your bike. They are particularly recommended for young children. Ultimately, wearing a helmet is a question of individual choice and parents need to make that choice for their children.

A bell is a must for considerate cyclists. A friendly tinkle warns that you are approaching, but never assume others can hear you.

LOCKING YOUR BIKE

Unless you are sitting right next to your bike when you stop for refreshments, it is worth locking it, preferably to something immovable like a post, fence or railings (or a bike stand, of course). If nothing else, lock it to a companion's bike. Bike theft is more common in towns and cities, and if you regularly leave your bike on the streets, it is important to invest in a good-quality lock and to lock and leave your bike in a busy, well-lit location.

GETTING TO THE START OF A RIDE

The best rides are often those that you can do right from your doorstep, maximizing time on your bike and reducing travelling time. If you need to travel to the start of the ride, have you thought about catching a train?

FINDING OUT MORE – WWW.SUSTRANS.ORG.UK

Use the Sustrans website to find out where you can cycle to from home or while you are away on holiday, and browse through a whole host of other useful information.
Visit www.sustrans.org.uk

MAKING THE MOST OF YOUR BIKE

Making a few simple adjustments to your bike will make your ride more enjoyable and comfortable:

- **Saddle height:** raise or lower it so that you have good contact with your pedals (to make the most of your leg power) and so that you can always put a reassuring foot on the ground.
- **Saddle position:** getting the saddle in the right place will help you get the most from your pedal power without straining your body.
- **Handlebars:** well-positioned handlebars are crucial for your comfort and important for control of your steering and brakes.

... BIKE MAINTENANCE

Like any machine, a bike will work better and last longer if you care for it properly. Get in the habit of checking your bike regularly – simple checks and maintenance can help you have hassle-free riding and avoid repairs.

- **Tools:** there are specialist tools for specific tasks, but all you need to get started are: a pump, an old toothbrush, lubricants and grease, cleaning rags, a puncture repair kit, tyre levers, allen keys, screwdrivers and spanners.

REGULAR CHECKS

- **Every week:** Check tyres, brakes, lights, handlebars and seat are in good order and tightly secured.
- **Every month:** Wipe clean and lubricate chain with chain oil.
  Wipe the dirt from wheels.
  Check tread on tyres.
  Check brake pads.
  Check gear and brake cables and make sure that gears are changing smoothly.
- **Every year:** Take your bike to an experienced mechanic for a thorough service.
- **Tip:** If in doubt, leave it to the professionals. Bike mechanics are much more affordable than car mechanics, and some will even collect the bike from your home and return it to you when all the work is done.

FIXING A PUNCTURE

Punctures don't happen often and are easy to fix yourself. If you don't fancy repairing a puncture on your journey, carry a spare inner tube and a pump so you can change the tube, then fix the puncture when you get home. If you don't mind repairing punctures when they happen, make sure you carry your repair kit and pump with you at all times. All puncture repair kits have full instructions with easy-to-follow pictures.

Alternatively, if you don't want to get your hands dirty, just visit your local bike shop and they will fix the puncture for you.

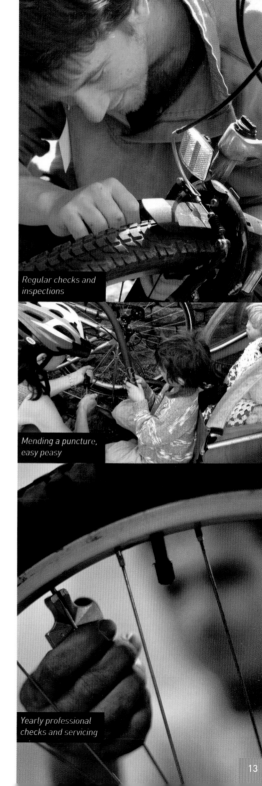

Regular checks and inspections

Mending a puncture, easy peasy

Yearly professional checks and servicing

PEREGRINE PATH (LLWYBR YR HEBOG)

The Peregrine Path, which straddles the England/Wales border, passes through some of the finest scenery in the UK. An excellent 3-mile (5km) traffic-free section is initially followed, largely alongside the River Wye, leading through the Upper Wye Gorge and on to Symonds Yat, where peregrine falcons may be seen. From there, the route continues, pleasantly, on minor roads to dramatically sited Goodrich, where you can visit the fortified baronial palace of Goodrich Castle.

Starting from the attractive town of Monmouth, there is a host of interesting historical sites to discover as you pedal effortlessly along.

Henry V, immortalized for his successful campaigns against the French in the 15th century, was born at Monmouth Castle, into one of England's most powerful noble families. However, at the time he was not in line for the throne and his birth was not precisely recorded; he was born in either 1386 or 1387.

The largely ruined Monmouth Castle is passed soon after leaving the 13th-century stone-gated Monnow Bridge. This bridge is unique in Britain, both for its design and state of preservation, and is matched by only two other similar structures in the whole of Europe.

ROUTE INFORMATION

National Route: This route is not part of the National Cycle Network.
Start: Old Monnow Bridge, Monmouth.
Finish: Church Pitch, Goodrich.

Distance: 8 miles (13km).
Grade: Easy.
Surface: Gravel path and tarmac.
Hills: None.

Medieval Monnow Bridge and gate

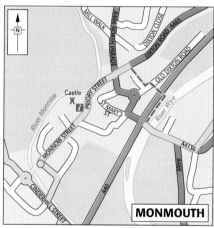
Goodrich Castle and the River Wye

MONMOUTH

YOUNG & INEXPERIENCED CYCLISTS
Suitable for novices and families with young children.

REFRESHMENTS
- Lots of choice in Monmouth and Goodrich.
- The Saracens Head pub, Symonds Yat East.
- Cafe at Goodrich Castle (seasonal opening).

THINGS TO SEE & DO
- Monmouth Castle: impressive ruins, with the Great Tower and Hall still standing; can be viewed for free from the parade ground of the Royal Monmouthshire Royal Engineers.
- RSPB Symonds Yat, Symonds Yat Rock: watch the cliffside nest of peregrine falcons from this limestone outcrop; from April to August, while the young are being reared, powerful telescopes are available, so you can see right into the nests; 07736 792511; www.rspb.org.uk
- Goodrich Castle: boasts one of the most complete sets of medieval domestic buildings surviving in any English castle; majestically sited, it commanded control of the River Wye into the valley of Symonds Yat; 0870 333 1181; www.english-heritage.org.uk

TRAIN STATIONS
None.

BIKE HIRE
- Pedalabikeaway, Monmouth: 01600 772821; www.pedalabikeaway.co.uk
- Pedalabikeaway Cycle Centre, Cannop Valley, near Coleford: 01594 860065; www.pedalabikeaway.co.uk
- Xtreme Wheels, Symonds Yat: 01600 716911; www.xtremewheels.co.uk

PEREGRINE PATH (LLWYBR YR HEBOG)

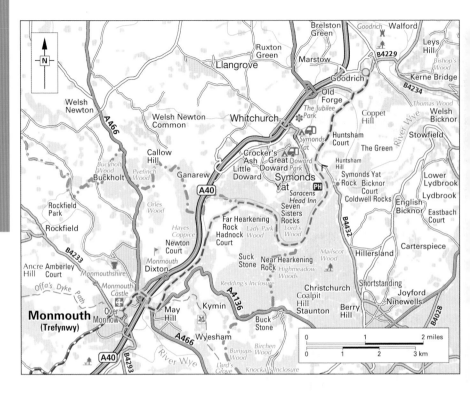

FURTHER INFORMATION

- To view or print National Cycle Network routes, visit www.sustrans.org.uk
- Maps for this area are available to buy from www.sustransshop.co.uk
- For further information on routes in Wales, visit www.routes2ride.org.uk/wales
- Monmouth Tourist Information: 01600 775257; www.visitwyevalley.com
- Forest of Dean Cycle Association: www.fodca.org.uk
- Wales Tourist Information: 0870 830 0306; www.visitwales.co.uk

ROUTE DESCRIPTION

Start from Old Monnow Bridge and cycle past Monmouth Castle. An underpass leads under the A40, then a road bridge leads over the River Wye. The tarmac surface provides easy cycling for 3 miles (5km) before giving way to a good gravel path. Cycle on to reach popular Symonds Yat rapids, where ancient hand-pull ferries still operate. Cyclists are advised to give way to walkers at all times and take special care here.

From Symonds Yat East you can walk to the Symonds Yat Rock for panoramic views over the Wye Valley and the Forest of Dean.

Stay on the east side of the river to join a minor road and follow this to cross a road bridge just to the south of Goodrich and continue to Church Pitch, where the route ends.

NEARBY CYCLE ROUTES

The Peregrine Path extends from Monmouth to Symonds Yat, following the line of the former Ross-on-Wye to Monmouth Railway.

There are a range of traffic-free options in the Forest of Dean, including the popular

The River Wye viewed from Symonds Yat Rock

waymarked Cycle Trail – an 11-mile (17.5km) family-friendly trail, which can be accessed from the Pedalabikeaway Cycle Centre near Coleford. You could also explore the winding country lanes.

For mountain bikers, there's a dedicated downhill and freeride area, in addition to a huge variety of easier forest trails.

Monmouth is linked by Regional Route 30 on minor roads with Cwmbran, where National Route 49 can be followed to Newport.

National Route 42, which runs from Chepstow to Hay-on-Wye via Abergavenny, passes to the west of Monmouth. It intersects with Regional Route 30 in Usk (Brynbuga).

NEWPORT TO CWMCARN

This is a lovely route on the Monmouthshire & Brecon Canal – a small network in south Wales – which is arguably the prettiest on the waterway system in the whole of the UK. This cycle ride follows the Crumlin Arm of the Monmouthshire Canal, which connected Crumlin and its tramways to the docks at Newport. The towpath is enhanced by artwork developed by schoolchildren and local community groups – a far cry from the days when the canal and surroundings were blackened by coal dust. Much of the canal has been lost but there are plans to make the southern end navigable again as far as Newport.

As you near Crosskeys, the Ebbw Valley, through which the canal passes, becomes more dramatic, with wooded hills rising to 300m (1,000ft) on either side. Crosskeys itself is a traditional South Wales Valleys community, with a strong coal-mining heritage. The route continues to Cwmcarn Forest. Once a mining area, Cwmcarn is now a beautiful mature forest of larch and pine.

The forest has an informative visitor centre and is home to the Twrch Mountain Bike Trail. Although not for the inexperienced, this superb single-track trail leads out from the forest to the open ridge tops, to give panoramic views of the Bristol Channel and the surrounding hills.

ROUTE INFORMATION

National Route: 47
Start: Riverfront Theatre and Arts Centre, Newport.
Finish: Visitor Centre, Cwmcarn Forest.

Distance: 9 miles (14.5km).
Grade: Easy.
Surface: Mostly tarmac.
Hills: Gentle incline, growing steep at Fourteen Locks, and a final climb to the visitor centre.

Brecon and Monmouth Canal

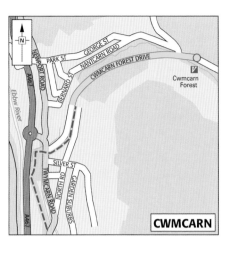

'Steel Wave' by Peter Fink

YOUNG & INEXPERIENCED CYCLISTS

Suitable for families with young children and novices.

REFRESHMENTS

- Lots of choice in Newport, including the Tom Jones-themed Bombay Bicycle Club.
- Various options in Crosskeys.
- Cafe at Cwmcarn Forest Visitor Centre.

THINGS TO SEE & DO

- Newport Museum & Art Gallery: displays on local history, the natural sciences and archaeology, with particularly impressive collections from the Roman town of Caerwent; the important story of the Chartist Uprising of 1839 is well illustrated; 01633 656656; www.newport.gov.uk
- Fourteen Locks Canal Centre, Newport:

A tricky section of the nearby Twrch Trail

BIKE HIRE
- Fourteen Locks Canal Centre: 01633 892167; www.fourteenlocks.co.uk

FURTHER INFORMATION
- To view or print National Cycle Network routes, visit www.sustrans.org.uk
- Maps for this area are available to buy from www.sustransshop.co.uk
- For further information on routes in Wales, visit www.routes2ride.org.uk/wales
- Newport Tourist Information: 01633 842962; www.visitwyevalley.com
- Wales Tourist Information: 0870 830 0306; www.visitwales.co.uk

ROUTE DESCRIPTION
From the Riverfront Theatre and Arts Centre in Newport, follow Route 47 initially alongside the River Usk. The valley and the surrounding drainage area have seen countless invasions – Wye Valley and the Vale of Usk have the greatest density of castles per square mile in Britain.

At the M4, Route 47 continues west, passing under the motorway before climbing steeply towards the Fourteen Locks Canal Centre. The cyclepath follows the towpath of the Monmouthshire & Brecon Canal to Crosskeys, where Route 47 branches west. Keep straight on here, following the canal, which leads to a road to the Cwmcarn Forest Visitor Centre.

a system of ponds, channels and tunnels, rising 42m (138ft) in just half a mile (0.8km); 01633 894802; www.fourteenlocks.co.uk
- **Newport Wetlands Reserve, Newport:** wealth of wetland birds, which thrive on the reed beds, saline lagoons, wet grassland and scrub; also an excellent place to see orchids, butterflies, dragonflies and otters; 01633 636363; www.rspb.org.uk
- **Sirhowy Valley Country Park, near Crosskeys:** ramble through the Flatwoods Meadows Local Nature Reserve or visit the restored Penllwyn Tramroad Bridge, complete with original stone sleepers; 01495 270991; www.caerphilly.gov.uk

TRAIN STATIONS
Newport; Rogerstone; Risca and Pontymister; Crosskeys.

NEARBY CYCLE ROUTES
The Newport to Cwmcarn route shares the start of its route with the Celtic Trail High Level Route (National Route 47). This is one option on the Celtic Trail, a long-distance route from Fishguard to Chepstow. The high-level route is ideal for those seeking both adventure and tranquillity.

In Newport, to the south of the Riverfront Theatre and Arts Centre, Route 47 links with the more coast-orientated Celtic Trail Low Level Route (Route 4). In south Wales, Route 4

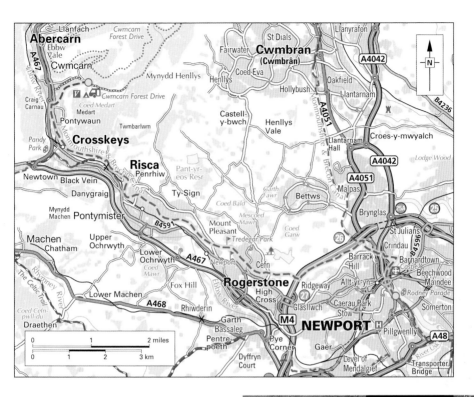

can be followed from Chepstow, through Newport, to Swansea, via Pontypridd. It offers the opportunity to experience the diversity of Welsh culture, history and natural beauty on canal towpaths, disued railways and quiet country lanes.

The Torfaen Leisure Route (Routes 49 and 492) runs the length of the County Borough of Torfaen, from Blaenavon in the north to Cwmbran in the south. The route in full extends for 18 miles (29km). In the south, it follows the Monmouthshire & Brecon Canal towpath (see page 22); in the north, it runs along the line of an old mineral railway (see page 38). Note that horse-riders also use the stretch of route from Wainfelin, Pontypool to Garn Lakes, Blaenavon. The southern end of the Torfaen Leisure Route links with Route 47, close to Newport train and bus stations.

Dragonfly sculpture by Joanne Risley

MONMOUTHSHIRE & BRECON CANAL

Enjoy a tranquil outing, pedalling with the greatest of ease from Newport, Wales' newest city, to Pontypool. A short riverside cyclepath by the Usk soon joins the Monmouthshire & Brecon Canal towpath, which leads almost effortlessly to an old canal basin at Pontypool.

Two canals used to run north and west from Newport – one to Pontypool and one to Newbridge. Both have fallen into disrepair but the towpaths are still largely intact. Canalside cycling, of course, presents some of the finest cycling in the country, and this route is no exception. As you progress, the landscape becomes more dramatic, with hills, such as Mynydd Maen (472m/1,548ft), making their presence felt. Further north lie the larger Y Mynyddoedd Duon, the aptly named Black Mountains.

The canal was built to connect with a large network of tramways, which transported limestone, coal and iron ore – the raw products hewn from the ancient landscape. The first 11-mile (17.5km) section of the canal was built between 1792 and 1796, to connect Newport to Pontnewnydd, which lies to the north of Pontypool. The rest of the canal, from Pontypool to Brecon, opened subsequently in 1812. Alas, the canals were superseded by the railways, and by 1850 the entire canal network was in decline. In 1962, the canals were abandoned and parts of these once revolutionary waterways were filled in.

ROUTE INFORMATION

National Routes: 47, 49, 492
Start: Riverfront Theatre and Arts Centre, Newport.
Finish: Pontymoile Canal Basin, Pontypool.
Distance: 9 miles (14.5km).
Grade: Easy.
Surface: Mainly tarmac.
Hills: Gentle incline from south to north.

YOUNG & INEXPERIENCED CYCLISTS

Ideal for novices and families with young children.

REFRESHMENTS

- Lots of choice in Newport, including the Tom Jones-themed Bombay Bicycle Club.
- Lots of choice in Cwmbran.
- Cafe in an old canal boat at Pontymoile Canal Basin.

THINGS TO SEE & DO

- **Newport Museum & Art Gallery:** displays on local history, the natural sciences and archaeology, with particularly impressive collections from the Roman town of

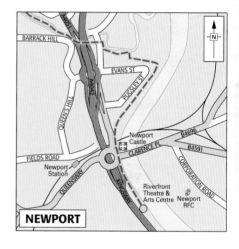

NEWPORT

Caerwent; the important story of the Chartist Uprising of 1839 is well illustrated; 01633 656656; www.newport.gov.uk
- **Fourteen Locks Canal Centre, Newport:** a system of ponds, channels and tunnels, rising 42m (138ft) in just half a mile (0.8km); 01633 894802; www.fourteenlocks.co.uk
- **Newport Wetlands Reserve, Newport:** wealth of wetland birds, which thrive on the

Canalside cycling offers level paths and pretty scenery

reed beds, saline lagoons, wet grassland and scrub; also an excellent place to see orchids, butterflies, dragonflies and otters; 01633 636363; www.rspb.org.uk

- **Pontypool Park, Pontypool:** locally known as the People's Park; several historical features, including an Italian Garden and an ice house; facilities include a children's play area; 01495 766754; www.torfaen.gov.uk

TRAIN STATIONS

Newport; Cwmbran; Pontypool & New Inn.

BIKE HIRE

- **Fourteen Locks Canal Centre:** 01633 892167; www.fourteenlocks.co.uk

FURTHER INFORMATION

- To view or print National Cycle Network routes, visit www.sustrans.org.uk
- Maps for this area are available to buy from www.sustransshop.co.uk
- For further information on routes in Wales, visit www.routes2ride.org.uk/wales
- **Newport Tourist Information:** 01633 842962;

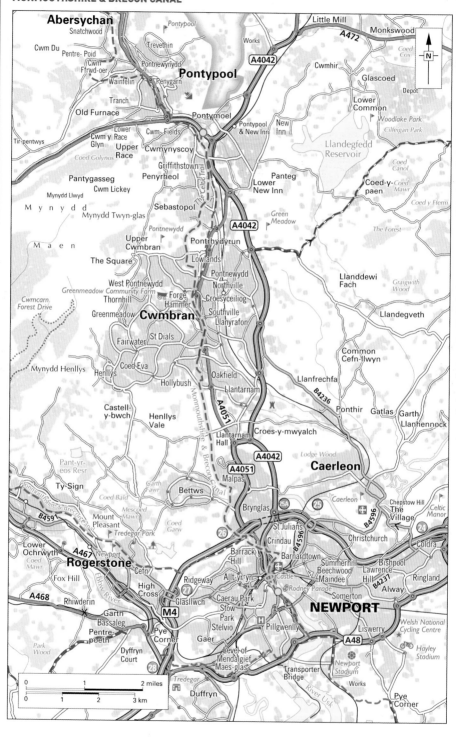

Along the Monmouthshire & Brecon Canal

www.visitwyevalley.com
- **Wales Tourist Information:** 0870 830 0306;
  www.visitwales.co.uk

ROUTE DESCRIPTION

From the Riverfront Theatre and Arts Centre in Newport, follow Route 47 initially alongside the River Usk. The valley and the surrounding drainage area have seen countless invasions – Wye Valley and the Vale of Usk have the most castles per square mile in Britain.

At the M4, take Route 49 north. There is an excellent wide tarmac towpath all the way to the finish point at the Pontymoel Canal Basin.

NEARBY CYCLE ROUTES

The Monmouthshire & Brecon Canal route shares the start of its route with the Celtic Trail High Level Route (National Route 47). This is part of the long-distance Fishguard to Chepstow route crossing Wales at its widest point, on a route packed with interest. The high-level route is both thrilling and peaceful.

The Monmouthshire & Brecon Canal route links with the more coastal Celtic Trail Low Level Route (National Route 4). In south Wales, Route 4 runs from Chepstow, through Newport, to Swansea, via Pontypridd. It offers the chance to experience the diversity of Welsh culture, history and natural beauty on canal towpaths, disused railways and quiet country lanes.

From Pontypool, you can continue north, on Route 492, to the Garn Lakes at Blaenavon. Part of the Torfaen Leisure Route, this provides a totally traffic-free cycling experience, following the line of an old mineral railway.

CLYDACH GORGE

Abergavenny's narrow streets are testimony to the town's long history, linked to the fortunes of its ruined 11th-century castle. The town is surrounded by mountains, most notably Blorenge, Ysgyryd Fawr (the Skirrid) and the Sugar Loaf, the latter rising to almost 610m (2,000ft) to the northwest of the town. The Usk Valley represents a real dividing line between the Brecon Beacons National Park and the lush green pastures grazed by sheep to the north and the old industrial heritage of the Welsh Valleys to the south, dominated by rows of terraced houses rising in ranks above the valley floors where the old coal mines were once worked by local men. Passing high above Clydach Gorge/ Ceunant Clydach, and following the line of the former Merthyr, Tredegar and Abergavenny Railway, the almost entirely traffic-free route runs between Llanfoist, just to the south of Abergavenny, and Brynmawr. The Clydach Gorge route has taken more than two decades to complete and marks the beginning of the Heads of Valleys route from Abergavenny to Neath. It also forms a key part of the Valleys Cycle Network, which will be developed over the coming years.

ROUTE INFORMATION
National Route: 46
Start: Llanfoist, southwest of Abergavenny.
Finish: East side of Brynmawr, at the roundabout at the junction of the A465, A467 and A4047.
Distance: 8 miles (13km).

Grade: Moderate.
Surface: Tarmac or gravel.
Hills: Steady climbs with a short, steep climb after Gilwern train station.

YOUNG & INEXPERIENCED CYCLISTS
Traffic-free route, with one short, steep, quiet lane section. There is a busy road crossing to get to the centre of Brynmawr.

REFRESHMENTS
None.

THINGS TO SEE & DO
- Views of beautiful Clydach Gorge lined with stately beech trees.
- **Monmouthshire & Brecon Canal:** 35-mile (56km) canal, which winds through peaceful countryside from Brecon, south to Cwmbran; www.waterscape.com
- **Blaenavon Industrial Landscape:** a World Heritage Site, conserving the area that, from the mid-18th century, was instrumental in the development of the iron and coal industries in the UK; www.world-heritage-blaenavon.org.uk
- Big Pit National Coal Museum, Blaenavon: 01495 790311; www.museumwales.ac.uk

Medieval Abergavenny Castle

View across Abergavenny

TRAIN STATIONS
Abergavenny.

BUSES
The Beacons Bus carries cyclists and runs on Sundays and Bank Holidays (summer only), from Cardiff to the Brecon Beacons National Park; www.cyclebreconbeacons.com

BIKE HIRE
• Bike Base Wales, Abergavenny: 01873 855999; www.bikebasewales.com

FURTHER INFORMATION
• To view or print National Cycle Network routes, visit www.sustrans.org.uk
• Maps for this area are available to buy from www.sustransshop.co.uk
• For more information on routes in Wales, visit www.routes2ride.org.uk/wales
• Abergavenny Tourist Information: 01873 854823; www.visitabergavenny.co.uk
• Wales Tourist Information: 0870 830 0306; www.visitwales.co.uk

ROUTE DESCRIPTION
The railway path starts at the car park on the west edge of Llanfoist, on the B4269, and from here you simply follow the signs for National Route 46 up the hill. Sustrans volunteer Rangers have also signed an excellent link from Abergavenny train station, so if you are arriving by train, turn right on exiting the station and follow Route 46 to Llanfoist.

On leaving the car park, the route climbs steadily and crosses the B4246 via the ingenious bridge designed by Christopher Wallis; his father was Barnes Wallis, the famous scientist, engineer and inventor of the bouncing bomb, as used in the 'Dambusters' raid of World War II. The route then crosses over the Monmouthshire & Brecon Canal, another great feat of engineering, and on to Govilon, where it crosses the road at the old train station. The next section passes through railway cuttings and woodland, and has good views out over the Usk Valley.

On arriving at Gilwern train station, where the old platform still exists, the route leaves the railway for a short time and follows quiet lanes. Care should be taken on this section because it includes a very steep, short climb. However, your effort is rewarded by a spectacular traffic-free route of 3 miles (5km). Once back on the old railway, carry on up to Clydach, where the route passes over a stone viaduct, and the industrial past of the area is in evidence. Cross the road again in Clydach village, and enter the Cwm Clydach Site of Special Scientific Interest (SSSI), where there are rare orchids and other plants of national significance. After coming out of this woodland section, stop and enjoy the fantastic views of Clydach Gorge and the Black Mountains.

The next section looks unfinished because the route is on a grass-covered railway track bed; it contains grassland fungi of rare international importance, so the route has been left untouched to preserve it. The route winds onwards, eventually arriving on the outskirts of Brynmawr. Sustrans plans to link the end of the route to the town centre but this has not yet been achieved, so if you are heading into Brynmawr, please take care when crossing the very busy road. Almost no pedalling is needed on the return journey and the views are superb.

NEARBY CYCLE ROUTES
National Route 46 links Abergavenny to Hereford. National Route 42 goes south to Chepstow and Usk and north to Hay-on-Wye via Gospel Pass. At Hay-on-Wye, Route 42 links to National Route 8 and together they form the long-distance route Lôn Las Cymru. National Route 492 and then National Route 49 go via a traffic-free route (see page 38) on lanes and B roads from Blaenavon to Newport.

Cycling is permitted on some sections of the Monmouthshire & Brecon Canal (see page 22), which runs from Brecon to Cwmbran (see www.waterscape.com for details).

Atop Clydach Gorge Viaduct

Clydach Gorge waterfall

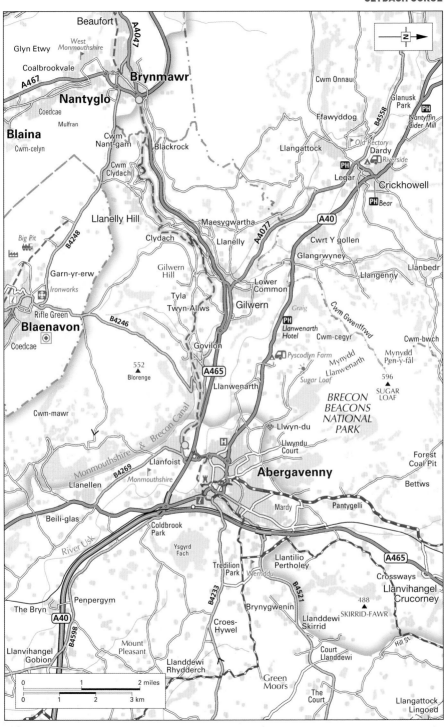

LLANHILLETH TO ABERTILLERY

This route starts at Llanhilleth station in a scenic narrow valley that was once scarred by mining. Dominating the valley to the south is the Miners Institute. Rows of miners' terraced houses, once visited by the Prince of Wales in 1936 to show support for an area that was one of the hardest hit in the Depression, are squeezed into the valley floor.

The River Ebbw runs through the valley. Previously known locally as the River Stinky, it was once the colour of rust and devoid of wildlife due to pollution from Ebbw Vale steelworks further north, but it is now clean and home to fish and otters.

After passing through the rows of terraced houses, you will ride alongside the River Ebbw to Aberbeeg. This is the point where the Ebbw splits into the Ebbw Fawr and Ebbw Fach. Aberbeeg was once a thriving town; home of a brewery and a railway yard. Now it is the start of a new traffic-free route. The path passes through a beautiful wooded valley where the distinctive blue-and-white flash of jays are often seen, and, in June, wild strawberries grow. Look out for *Guardian*, the enormous and imposing statue of a miner by Sebastian Boyesen. It was erected in 2010 near the site of Six Bells Colliery to commemorate the 50th anniversary of the mining disaster that killed 45 men in 1960.

View over the town of Abertillery

ROUTE INFORMATION
National Route: 465 (Ebbw Fach Trail)
Start: Llanhilleth train station.
Finish: Abertillery Park.
Distance: 4 miles (6km).
Grade: Easy.
Surface: Tarmac.
Hills: Mainly flat.

YOUNG & INEXPERIENCED CYCLISTS
Ideal for young and inexperienced riders, especially the traffic-free section near *Guardian*.

REFRESHMENTS
• Bakery in Llanhilleth.
• Several cafes in Abertillery.

THINGS TO SEE & DO
• **Llanhilleth Miners Institute:** the 'Stute' provides a vibrant link with the industrial past of the Ebbw Valley. Built in 1906, this Grade II listed building was fully restored in 2008.
• *Guardian:* this huge statue of a miner was erected to commemorate the 50th anniversary of the 1960 Six Bells mining disaster. The statue is made from over 20,000 individual ribbons of corten steel.
• **Abertillery & District Museum:** discover the history and heritage of the Abertillery area. This place will bring back memories for older visitors and offers plenty to entertain children too; 01495 211140; www.abertilleryanddistrictmuseum.org.uk

TRAIN STATIONS
Llanhilleth.

BIKE HIRE
• **PS Cycles Abercarn:** 01495 246555; www.pscycles.co.uk

FURTHER INFORMATION
• To view or print National Cycle Network routes, visit www.sustrans.org.uk

Mosaic mural in Abertillery underpass

• Maps for this area are available to buy from www.sustransshop.co.uk
• For more information on routes in Wales, visit www.routes2ride.org.uk/wales
• **Wales Tourist Information:** 0870 830 0306

ROUTE DESCRIPTION
On leaving the station, cross over the railway and turn right at the Miners Institute into Meadow Street. Travelling north, after a mile (1.6km), pass under the railway to join a traffic-free path. Look out for *Guardian* on the left and make a detour to get a closer look. The path then joins Castle Street and passes through a supermarket car park. Care should be taken here! Look out for the murals that depict Abertillery life and use the underpass to join Carlyle Street; this leads to the finish in Abertillery Park.

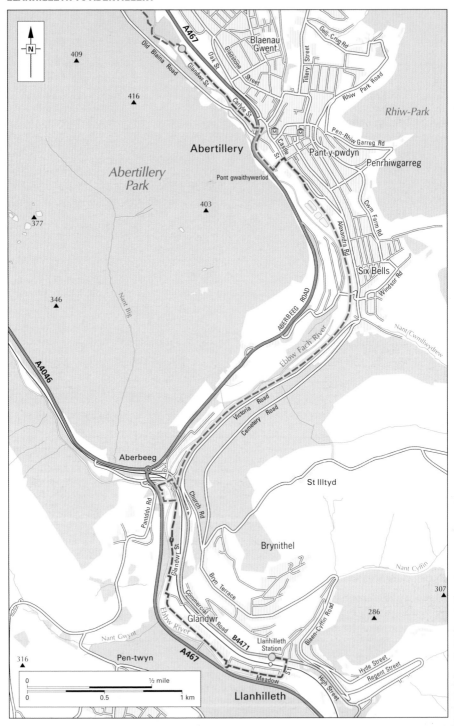

St Illtyd churchyard

NEARBY CYCLE ROUTES

National Route 465, the Ebbw Fach Trail, carries on north from Abertillery Park to join National Route 46 at Brynmawr. Route 46 goes west to link with the Taff Trail, National Route 8, at Merthyr. It also turns east to Abergavenny where it joins Lôn Las Cymru, National Route 42, as well as the Monmouthshire & Brecon Canal (cycling permitted). The canal can be followed north to Brecon and south to join Route 49 at Pontypool.

The enormous 'Guardian' memorial

THREE PARCS RIDE

Traffic-free cycle rides are a delight at any time of year but this one is an absolute joy in the spring, when the three parks through which this route passes are filled with colour and the heady scent of pollen. It wasn't always thus: the route leads by rivers that once ran black with coal dust. The regeneration of this post-industrial landscape has been hugely successful. Today, woodlands and wildlife, including otters and peregrine falcons, are once again thriving in these beautiful Welsh Valleys.

The ride begins with a lovely, family-friendly stretch through the Sirhowy Valley Country Park, following one of the most enjoyable sections of the entire Celtic Trail. Further on, the route crosses the Hengoed Viaduct – a 260m (853ft) high, 16-arch listed viaduct, which spans the Rhymney Valley. Built in 1857, it completed a rail route that linked all the valleys from Pontypool to Swansea. *Wheel of Drams*, an 8m (26ft) high sculpture known as 'Drams', stands proudly by the cyclepath here.

Continuing up the valley, you pass through Parc Penallta, a former colliery site, which is well worth exploring. Soon after, the route passes the town of Nelson, so-named after a visit from Lord Nelson in 1803, two years before the Battle of Trafalgar. The former mining village is now a designated conservation area and makes a good spot for a break.

At Trelewis, Route 47 is left for the final approach up the Taff Bargoed Valley, to pass through the pretty Parc Taff Bargoed.

Metal sculpture at Parc Penallta

ROUTE INFORMATION

National Route: 47
Start: Visitor Centre, Sirhowy Valley Country Park, near Crosskeys.
Finish: Summit Centre, Taff Bargoed.
Distance: 11 miles (17.5km).
Grade: Moderate.
Surface: Tarmac and gravel.
Hills: Mainly flat.

YOUNG & INEXPERIENCED CYCLISTS

Ideal for families with fit children – the route is traffic-free but there are four road crossings.

REFRESHMENTS

- Options at Crosskeys, Hengoed, Nelson and other points en route.
- Cafe at the Summit Centre, Taff Bargoed.

THINGS TO SEE & DO

- Sirhowy Valley Country Park, near Crosskeys: ramble through the Flatwoods Meadows Local Nature Reserve or visit the

restored Penllwyn Tramroad Bridge, complete with original stone sleepers; 01495 270991; www.caerphilly.gov.uk
- **Ynys Hywel Farm, Sirhowy Valley Country Park, Wattsville:** working hill farm, with Welsh black and belted Galloway cattle, badger-faced sheep, Tamworth pigs and a variety of chickens and ducks; 01495 270991; www.caerphilly.gov.uk
- **Parc Penallta Country Park, near Ystrad Mynach:** regenerated colliery, with panoramic views from the High Point Observatory; interesting collection of outdoor artworks; 01443 816853; www.caerphilly.gov.uk
- **Summit Centre, Parc Taff Bargoed:** adventure activity centre, with one of the largest indoor facilities in the UK; home to one of Europe's largest climbing walls; 01443 710749; www.summitcentre.co.uk

TRAIN STATIONS

Crosskeys; Hengoed; Quaker's Yard.

BIKE HIRE

- **Fourteen Locks Canal Centre:** 01633 892167; www.fourteenlocks.co.uk

FURTHER INFORMATION

- To view or print National Cycle Network routes, visit www.sustrans.org.uk
- Maps for this area are available to buy from www.sustransshop.co.uk
- For further information on routes in Wales, visit www.routes2ride.org.uk/wales
- **Caerphilly Tourist Information:** 029 2088 0011; www.visitcaerphilly.com
- **Wales Tourist Information:** 0870 830 0306; www.visitwales.co.uk

ROUTE DESCRIPTION

From the Sirhowy Valley Country Park Visitor Centre, follow National Route 47 on a traffic-free cyclepath. After some 2 miles (3km), the path climbs up the Sirhowy Valley and crosses the Hengoed Viaduct.

Pedal on through Parc Penallta, enjoying the traffic-free cyclepath. Further on, Route 47 leads along Trelewis High Street on a cyclepath and across a footbridge over the cascades of the Taff Bargoed River. At this point, the ride leaves Route 47, to continue north to Parc Taff Bargoed. Passing through pleasant woodland, you arrive at the Summit Centre.

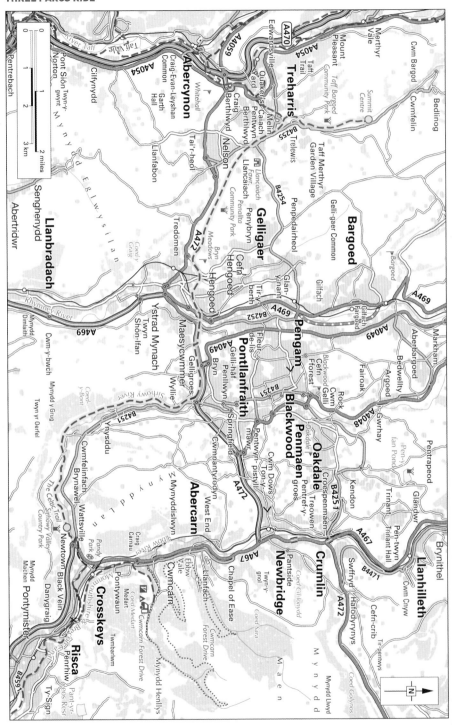

NEARBY CYCLE ROUTES

This ride is part of the High Level Route (National Route 47), an option on the Celtic Trail which runs from Chepstow to Fishguard. It is a key route within the Valleys Cycle Network. From Quaker's Yard, Route 47 follows an exciting and remote quiet road to Neath, and in the opposite direction from Cwmcarn near Crosskeys to Newport (see page 18).

The Taff Trail (Route 8), Wales' longest established cycle route, can also be joined at Quaker's Yard. This superb, predominantly traffic-free trail stretches for 55 miles (88km) from the market town of Brecon to Cardiff. Along the way, it crosses the Brecon Beacons and follows the Taff Vale, via Merthyr Tydfil and Pontypridd.

Cwmcarn Mountain Bike Centre, north of Crosskeys, has a red-graded 11-mile (17.5km) single-track loop and the black-graded

'Wheel of Drams' by Andy Hazel at Hengoed

1.2-mile (2km) Y Mynydd downhill track for experienced riders, with a year-round lift for the ascent. There's also an excellent freeride park (www.mbwales.com).

Route 47 crosses over this bridge

A TRIP TO THE COALFACE – PONTYPOOL TO BLAENAVON

Discover one of the principal centres of the Industrial Revolution, where the face of the world was changed. At the edge of the Brecon Beacons National Park, the town of Pontypool grew when an ironworks was established there in the late 16th century. Further up the valley, at Blaenavon, the end point of the route, this once small village played a significant part in the history of the Industrial Revolution during the 19th century.

This traffic-free route follows a disused railway line to Blaenavon, now protected as a World Heritage Site. Along the way, there are lovely valley views and a pretty stretch through broadleaf woodland to reach the heather-clad moors.

At the World Heritage Site, you can feel the presence of the past, where men toiled to make this area one of the early powerhouses of the world. Many of the schools, shops and chapels built in those early days are still standing: there are 17 listed buildings, including Blaenavon Ironworks, one of the best-preserved examples of 18th-century ironworks in Western Europe. Built in 1788, the ironworks reached their zenith in the 1820s. A viewing platform allows visitors to see the blast furnaces, casting house, water balance lift and workers' houses. Also, at the award-winning Big Pit: National Coal Museum, you can experience going underground in a real colliery.

ROUTE INFORMATION
National Route: 492
Start: Hanbury Road, Pontypool
(near the A472/A4043 roundabout).
Finish: Big Pit, Blaenavon.

Distance: 9 miles (14.5km).
Grade: Easy.
Surface: Tarmac.
Hills: Gradual incline.

All aboard the Pontypool & Blaenavon Railway

YOUNG & INEXPERIENCED CYCLISTS

Suitable for novices and families with young children. Note that horse-riders also use this stretch of the route.

REFRESHMENTS

- Lots of choice in Pontypool.
- Various options in Blaenavon.

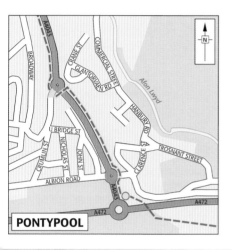

THINGS TO SEE & DO

- **Blaenavon Ironworks:** in the early 19th century this was one of the most advanced ironworks in the world; learn about iron making and the hard lives led by the workers and their families; 01495 792615; www.visitblaenavon.co.uk
- **Pontypool & Blaenavon Railway, Blaenavon:** highest-standard gauge preserved railway in Wales and England, travelling through the wild and dramatic landscape beneath the Coity Mountain; 01495 792263; www.pontypool-and-blaenavon.co.uk
- **Blaenavon World Heritage Site:** preserved iron- and coal-producing area from the 19th century, with coal and ore mines, quarries, railway, furnaces and workers' homes; 01495 742333; www.visitblaenavon.co.uk
- **Big Pit: National Coal Museum, Blaenavon:** a real coal mine and one of Britain's leading mining museums; go 91m (299ft) underground with a miner and see what life was like for the thousands of men who worked at the coal face; 01495 790311; www.museumwales.ac.uk

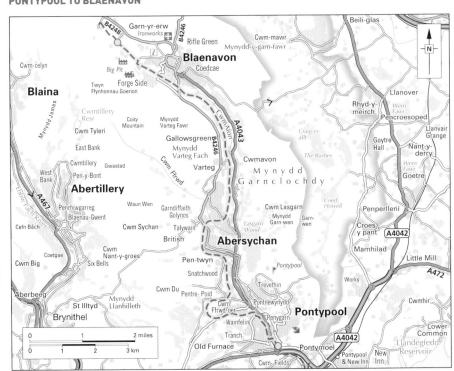

Industrial remains add scenic interest

TRAIN STATIONS
Pontypool & New Inn.

BIKE HIRE
- Mountain Tours, Blaenavon:
  01495 793123;www.chunkofwales.co.uk

FURTHER INFORMATION
- To view or print National Cycle Network routes, visit www.sustrans.org.uk
- Maps for this area are available to buy from www.sustransshop.co.uk
- For further information on routes in Wales, visit www.routes2ride.org.uk/wales
- Pontypool Tourist Information:
  www.visittorfaen.co.uk
- Blaenavon World Heritage Centre:
  01495 742333; www.visitblaenavon.co.uk
- Wales Tourist Information:
  0870 830 0306; www.visitwales.co.uk

ROUTE DESCRIPTION
Following the line of an old mineral railway, part of the Torfaen Leisure Route, this ride provides a totally traffic-free cycling experience. Starting from Pontypool's Hanbury Road, follow the National Route 492 signs to the north. The path climbs steadily as it heads north from Pontypool through Abersychan to Blaenavon, soon entering a long stretch of lovely broadleaf woodland, with fine views to the east across the valley of Afon Llwyd.

Leave the route in Blaenavon to explore the World Heritage Site attractions before continuing to the Big Pit: National Coal Museum. Big Pit is a living, breathing reminder of the coal industry in Wales and the people and society it created.

From there, you could easily extend the route a short distance up to the Garn Lakes, where there's a welcoming pub. Don't worry about the cycle back – having climbed more than 200m (656ft) up to Blaenavon, you'll be pleased to find the return journey is a lot easier!

NEARBY CYCLE ROUTES
The Torfaen Leisure Route (National Routes 49 and 492) runs the length of the County Borough of Torfaen, from Blaenavon in the north to Cwmbran in the south, approximately 18 miles (29km). This route makes up the northern section; in the south, it follows the Monmouthshire & Brecon Canal towpath (see page 22).

The southern end of the Torfaen Leisure Route links with Route 47, close to Newport train and bus stations. Route 47 forms part of the Celtic Trail route, which runs from Fishguard to Chepstow, crossing Wales at its widest point, on an inland route that is packed with interest.

Big Pit: National Coal Museum

TREVITHICK TRAIL

Industrial heritage abounds on this stunning route. Passing through the Taff Vale, it follows mainly traffic-free cyclepaths, with some quiet road sections, along the Trevithick Trail, between Edwardsville and Merthyr Tydfil, and parts of the popular Taff Trail.

The Trevithick Trail is named after Cornish-born Richard Trevithick, known as the father of the railways. A visionary of the early Industrial Revolution, this multi-talented man died penniless yet, during his productive lifetime, he created the world's first steam-powered, load-hauling locomotive. In 1804, the Penydarren steam engine made history when it pulled 10 tonnes of iron bars from Merthyr Tydfil to Abercynon – a distance of 9 miles (14.5km). Today, the Trevithick Trail acknowledges the historic feat by following the line of that world-changing journey. Trevithick also created the first passenger-carrying steam road locomotive and the world's first fare-paying passenger railway.

The trail is as true to the original alignment as possible, though there are short hills and sections on quiet residential roads. Sweeping views of the mountains and the valley add to the experience as you pass through this former mining stronghold.

After Merthyr Tydfil, the Taff Trail leads on across the spectacular Cefn Coed Viaduct, following a disused railway line, to Pontsticill Reservoir in the uplifting Brecon Beacons National Park.

ROUTE INFORMATION

National Routes: 8, 477
Start: Navigation House pub, Abercynon.
Finish: North end of Pontsticill Reservoir.
Distance: 18 miles (29km).

Grade: Moderate.
Surface: Mostly tarmac.
Hills: Gentle incline from Abercynon to Merthyr Tydfil. From Merthyr, this becomes more pronounced.

Cefn Coed Viaduct

*Sculpture honouring
Richard Trevithick*

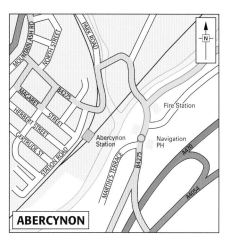

ABERCYNON

YOUNG & INEXPERIENCED CYCLISTS

Suitable for young families and novices, as the route is mostly traffic-free, with some sections on quiet roads. Care is required at the major road crossings.

REFRESHMENTS

- Lots of choice in urban centres en route.
- Refreshments at Brecon Mountain Railway.

THINGS TO SEE & DO

- **Pontygwaith Nature Reserve, near Quaker's Yard:** wildlife haven that can be explored on a network of paths; interpretation panels and information leaflets enhance the experience; 01685 377848; www.merthyr.gov.uk
- **Cyfarthfa Castle, Merthyr Tydfil:** grand castellated mansion, commissioned by iron tycoon William Crawshay; impressive monument from the Industrial Iron Age; 01685 727371; www.visitmerthyr.co.uk
- **Joseph Parry's Ironworker's Cottage, Merthyr Tydfil:** superb example of a skilled ironworker's cottage, where the famous Welsh composer, Dr Parry, was born; 01685 727371; www.museums.merthyr.gov.uk
- **Brecon Mountain Railway, Pontsticill:** historic steam railway, which runs alongside Pontsticill and Pentwyn Reservoirs and into the Brecon Beacons National Park; 01685 722988; www.breconmountainrailway.co.uk

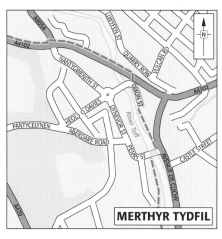

MERTHYR TYDFIL

TREVITHICK TRAIL

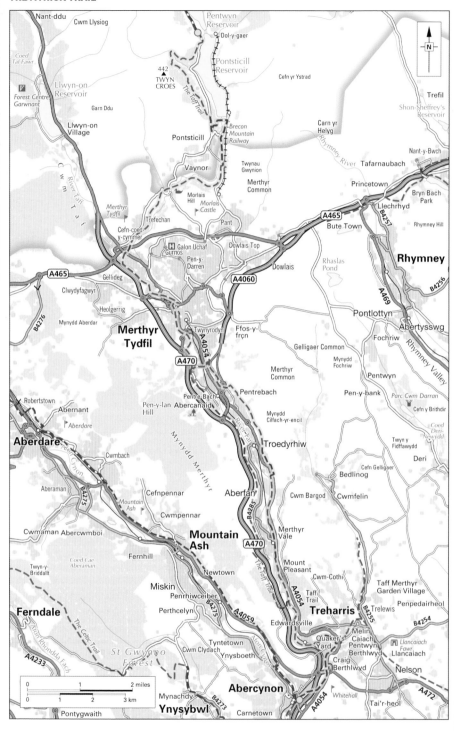

TRAIN STATIONS

Abercynon; Quaker's Yard; Merthyr Vale;
Troedyrhiw; Pentrebach; Merthyr Tydfil.

BIKE HIRE

- Cardiff Pedal Power, Cardiff:
  029 2039 0713; www.cardiffpedalpower.org
- The Summit Centre, Trelewis:
  01443 710749; www.summitcentre.co.uk

FURTHER INFORMATION

- To view or print National Cycle Network
  routes, visit www.sustrans.org.uk
- Maps for this area are available to buy from
  www.sustransshop.co.uk
- For further information on routes in Wales,
  visit www.routes2ride.org.uk/wales
- Merthyr Tydfil Tourist Information:
  01685 727474; www.merthyr.gov.uk
- Wales Tourist Information:
  0870 830 0306; www.visitwales.co.uk

ROUTE DESCRIPTION

From the Navigation House pub, which is
situated towards the end of the trail, follow
signs for National Route 8 upriver, along the
route of the original tram road, through
Quaker's Yard and up the Taff Vale.

Beyond Edwardsville, leave Route 8 to
follow Route 477. Trevithick Trail markers
highlight points of interest. At Merthyr Vale,
there's a short section on local roads and
access to shops. Further on, the route
crosses the A4054, where caution is required.

Carry on by Troedyrhiw, following signs
through a Co-op car park, a short section
by an industrial estate, and across the busy
A4060. Next, you enter a wonderful wooded
area. Pass over a small bridge and at the
next junction turn sharp left down to
Trevithick Tunnel. Carry on until you reach
the A4054 and then follow the signs to the
Taff Trail. From there, follow Route 8 north,
crossing the Cefn Coed Viaduct, along a
mixture of traffic-free cyclepaths and quiet

Pontsticill Reservoir

roads, to reach the north end of the
Pontsticill Reservoir.

NEARBY CYCLE ROUTES

The Trevithick Trail (National Route 477) is a
short section of historic trail that runs from
north of Edwardsville to the south of Merthyr
Tydfil. The trail runs parallel to the Taff Trail
(Route 8).

The Taff Trail (Route 8) is Wales' longest
established cycle route. This superb,
predominantly traffic-free trail stretches for 55
miles (88km) from the market town of Brecon
to Cardiff. Along the way, it crosses the Brecon
Beacons and follows the Taff Vale, via Merthyr
Tydfil and Pontypridd.

A section of the Celtic Trail High Level Route
(Route 47) is followed from Abercynon to
Quaker's Yard. The long-distance Celtic Trail
crosses Wales at its widest point, and is packed
with interest throughout its length.

The more coastal-orientated Celtic Trail Low
Level Route option (Route 4) can be accessed
at Pontypridd. In south Wales, this route can
be followed from Chepstow, through Newport,
to Swansea.

CYNON TRAIL – ABERCYNON TO HIRWAUN

The Cynon Trail, known in Welsh as the Taith Cynon, is one of the newest cycling trails to open in the country. Running along the natural corridor of the River Cynon, and between the nearby Taff and Celtic Trails (National Routes 8 and 47), it offers an excellent opportunity to cycle in this glorious part of south Wales and visit sites of recreational, historical and wildlife interest.

The route leads along sections of an old canal, constructed from the early 19th century, which runs parallel to the River Cynon for most of its length. An old railway line, which is also followed by the Cynon Trail, was built later as coal production increased in the valley. Many of the collieries were linked to the railway by branch lines and sidings. However, the economic viability of the canal, in common with the majority of canals at the time, was jeopardized by the arrival of the railway – the canal owners managed to withhold consent to build bridges over the canal until a court ruling in 1851.

This part of Wales is rich in waterfalls

ROUTE INFORMATION
National Route: 478
Start: Abercynon train station.
Finish: Cynon Terrace, Hirwaun.
Distance: 12 miles (19km).
Grade: Moderate.
Surface: Tarmac.
Hills: No major hills, although there is a gradual incline as you cycle up-valley.

YOUNG & INEXPERIENCED CYCLISTS
The traffic-free sections are suitable for families, provided care is taken at the road crossings and along temporary road sections.

REFRESHMENTS
- Various options in Abercynon, Mountain Ash (Aberpennar), Aberdare and Hirwaun.

THINGS TO SEE & DO
- **Dare Valley Country Park, near Aberdare:** multitude of walking trails with spectacular views, a fun family quest trail and an interactive visitor centre; 01685 874672; www.darevalleycountrypark.co.uk
- **Cynon Valley Museum & Gallery, Aberdare:** learn about the daily lives of past generations in the Cynon Valley; 01685 886729; www.cymg.co.uk
- **Brecon Beacons National Park:** encompasses remote wilderness, ancient woodlands, breathtaking waterfalls, caves, and windswept uplands; 01874 624437; www.breconbeacons.org

TRAIN STATIONS
Abercynon; Penrhiwceiber; Mountain Ash; Fernhill; Cwmbach; Aberdare.

BIKE HIRE
- **Cardiff Pedal Power, Cardiff:** 029 2039 0713; www.cardiffpedalpower.org

FURTHER INFORMATION
- To view or print National Cycle Network routes, visit www.sustrans.org.uk
- Maps for this area are available to buy from www.sustransshop.co.uk
- For further information on routes in Wales, visit www.routes2ride.org.uk/wales
- **Pontypridd Tourist Information:** 01443 490748; www.visitrct.co.uk
- **Wales Tourist Information:** 0870 830 0306; www.visitwales.co.uk

ROUTE DESCRIPTION
Note that two sections of the Cynon Trail are incomplete at the time of writing (detailed later), and the trail follows main roads. From Abercynon train station, follow the Cynon Trail

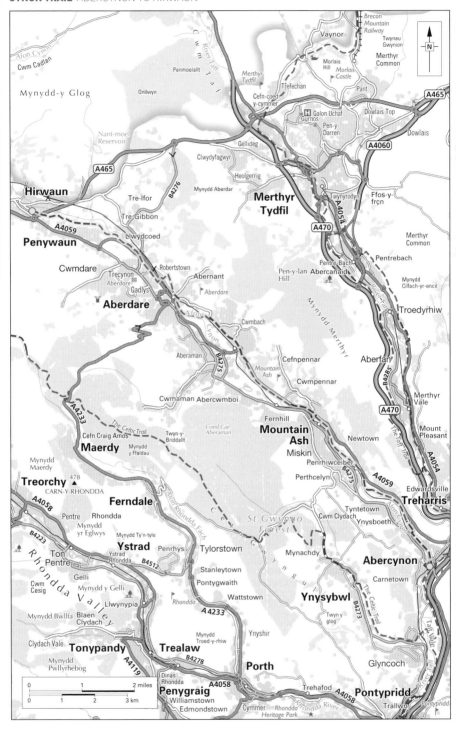

Terraced houses at Cwmdare

along the west side of the river. This part of the route is traffic-free. At the end of Park Road, turn right and then left into an industrial estate before following the trail along the east bank of the river.

Just before reaching Mountain Ash, the route crosses the river twice. After the second bridge turn immediately left to the first break in the route. Continue along New Road for about 500m – don't cross the river – to rejoin the route on a shared-use path alongside the road.

After a mile (1.6km), the route stops again at a petrol station. Rejoin the road (A4059) and go straight on at the next roundabout (Cwmbach station will be on your left). Follow this road, past an industrial estate, for 0.75 miles (1.2km), to rejoin the route, which soon passes under a low bridge alongside the old canal. At the next junction, turn left, passing under the railway line, and cycle on by the sports ground. Then go through the underpass (Aberdare train station is on the left) and carefully follow the signs to reach a bridge that takes you over the A4059 and then north along the ends of terraced houses. After crossing the B4276, carefully

follow the signs and cross the A4059 at a roundabout. The route then follows an old road and railway for the last 2.5 miles (4km) to Cynon Terrace, Hirwaun.

NEARBY CYCLE ROUTES

The Taff Trail (Route 8), Wales' longest established cycle route, links with the Cynon Trail in Abercynon. This superb, predominantly traffic-free trail stretches for 55 miles (88km) from the market town of Brecon to Cardiff. It is one of the most popular routes on the National Cycle Network. Along the way, it crosses the Brecon Beacons and follows the Taff Vale, via Merthyr Tydfil and Pontypridd.

The Penderyn Quarry Line can be followed from Hirwaun (Penyard Road) for some 1.5 miles (2.5km) to Penderyn.

The High Level Route option (Route 47) of the Celtic Trail, a long-distance route that runs from Chepstow to Fishguard, passes through Abercynon. To the east there is an excellent family-friendly, traffic-free section that runs from Trelewis and down the Sirhowy Valley to Sirhowy Country Park (see page 34).

CEFN CRIBWR – TONDU TO PYLE

This is a lovely ride for all the family along a predominantly wooded route, which runs through several vibrant nature reserves. There are Scheduled Ancient Monuments at either end: Tondu Ironworks at the start, and Cefn Cribwr Ironworks, near Pyle, at the end.

The route starts in the town of Tondu (Welsh for 'black sward'), which became established in the late 18th century as a coal-mining village to service the nearby Parc Slip colliery. From Tondu, you can branch off the main route to visit Tondu Iron Park – the most complete ironworks in Britain.

Back on the traffic-free route, you next reach the Parc Slip Nature Park, a wildlife oasis, where the route leads across wooden decking. A hundred years ago, this landscape was transformed by the coal workings. Today, it's home to hares, adders, great crested newts and 28 species of butterfly, with rare wading birds passing through during the migrating seasons. Although peaceful now, some locals still talk of a fatal explosion, probably caused by a hole in one of the workers' Davy lamps, which took the lives of 110 men and boys – the majority of the workforce – in 1892.

Halfway along the route you reach the high point, from where you can enjoy a gentle descent to Pyle, passing Bedford Park. The return journey can be made by train.

ROUTE INFORMATION

National Route: 4
Start: Tondu train station.
Finish: Pyle train station.
Distance: 7 miles (11km). Other options: Tondu to Bridgend 3 miles (5km); Tondu to Blackmill 3 miles (5km).
Grade: Easy.
Surface: Tarmac and gravel.
Hills: Gradual incline for the initial 2.5 miles (4km), followed by a descent into Pyle.

YOUNG & INEXPERIENCED CYCLISTS
Suitable for novices and families with young children.

REFRESHMENTS
- Picnic site and cafe (April to October) at Parc Slip Nature Park Visitor Centre.
- Lots of choice in Pyle.

THINGS TO SEE & DO
- **Tondu Iron Park:** the most complete ironworks in Britain, with coke ovens, kilns and engine houses; 01656 722315; www.bridgend.gov.uk
- **Parc Slip Nature Park, near Tondu:** wonderfully restored opencast mine and colliery coal tip, where you can admire flower-rich meadows and wetland sites; a visitor centre, run by the Wildlife Trust, details the local flora and fauna through interactive exhibitions; 01656 724100; www.welshwildlife.org
- **Bedford Park, near Pyle:** once an area of intense industrial activity, where iron was forged, now transformed into 40 acres of

European or brown hare on the alert

quiet woodlands, meadows, secret glades and green open spaces; 01656 725155; www.bridgend.gov.uk
- **Frog Wood Pond Local Nature Reserve, near Pyle:** haven for wildlife, including nuthatches, wood mice, common blue damselflies and palmate newts; known locally as Froggy Pond; 01656 643643; www.bridgend.gov.uk

TRAIN STATIONS
Tondu; Pyle.

BIKE HIRE
- **Afan Valley Bike Hire:** 01639 893661; www.afan-valley-bike-hire.com

FURTHER INFORMATION
- To view or print National Cycle Network routes, visit www.sustrans.org.uk
- Maps for this area are available to buy from www.sustransshop.co.uk
- For further information on routes in Wales, visit www.routes2ride.org.uk/wales
- **Bridgend Tourist Information:** 01656 654906; www.visitbridgend.com
- **Wales Tourist Information:** 0870 830 0306; www.visitwales.co.uk

Foxgloves grow in profusion in this region

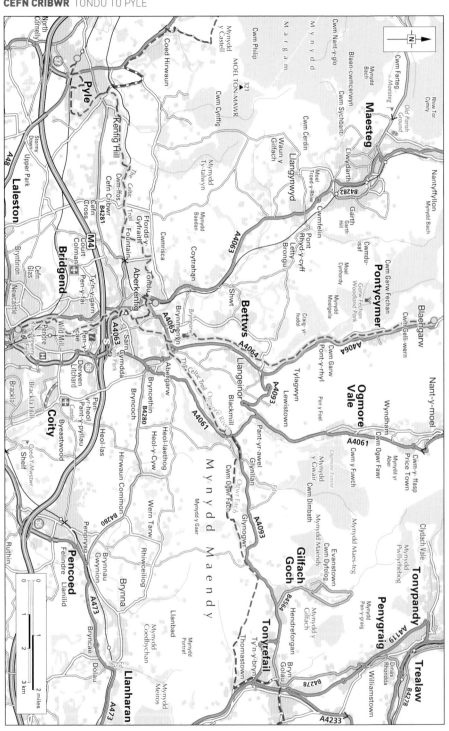

Tondu Ironworks

ROUTE DESCRIPTION

From Tondu train station, turn right along the A4065/Brynn Road to pick up the signs for National Route 4. These lead under a bridge and into a forest to join an old railway line following the route of the Duffryn, Llynfi & Porthcawl Railway, built to link the ironworks at Maesteg with the coast at Porthcawl. It's easy to follow the line all the way to the outskirts of Pyle, where you leave Route 4 to follow a local route to Pyle station. Many alternatives from Tondu are possible on the National Network, as shown on the map opposite. These include continuing south to Bridgend (largely traffic-free on Route 88) and northeast to Blackmill (completely traffic-free on Route 4) along the Ogmore Valley. The Garw Valley Community Route goes north from Tondu to Blaengarw.

NEARBY CYCLE ROUTES

The Tondu to Pyle route is part of the longer Celtic Trail Route (National Routes 4 and 47), which extends, as a linear trail, for 223 miles (359km) from Fishguard to Chepstow, broadly following the south coast. Route 4 runs between London and Fishguard, via Reading, Bath, Bristol, Newport, Swansea, Carmarthen, Tenby, Haverfordwest and St David's.

National Route 47 – the Celtic Trail High Level Route option – can be joined to the east of Swansea at Briton Ferry. From there, the initial section, along the Neath Canal, offers a great traffic-free ride to Tonna.

Afan Forest Park, east of Port Talbot (see page 54), offers mountain bikers single tracks through forest and exposed rocky double tracks on wide open hills (www.forestry.gov.uk).

PONTRHYDYFEN TO AFAN FOREST PARK

Afan Forest Park has become a centre of cycling excellence, with trails built to suit all abilities, from easy traffic-free routes with gentle gradients along the course of old railway lines in the valley to tough, single-track mountain bike challenges on the steep wooded valley sides.

This route takes in a gentle, traffic-free loop in the Afan Valley, where you can cycle all day to your heart's content on the numerous trails the area has to offer. There's a link up to Glyncorrwg village, too, once an important mining centre, which passes Glyncorrwg Ponds – the perfect place for a break.

Afan Forest Park has the fastest-growing mountain bike area in Britain and was rated by *Mountain Bike Rider* magazine as 'one of the top 10 places in the world to ride before you die'. However, you don't have to be a die-hard, armour-clad, downhill nut to enjoy the trails, as, thankfully, there's something for everyone here and plenty of family-friendly attractions to keep the little ones amused too.

A multi-million pound project is under way (part of the Lottery-funded Connect2 scheme run by Sustrans), connecting Port Talbot to Cwmafan and Afan Forest by a dedicated walking and cycling network.

ROUTE INFORMATION

National Routes: 887, 885
Start: Rhyslyn car park, Pontrhydyfen.
Finish: Afan Forest Park (also known as Afan Argoed Country Park).
Distance: 12 miles (19.5km).
Grade: Moderate.

Surface: Tarmac and gravel.
Hills: Easy valley cycle from Pontrhydyfen, followed by a climb to Glyncorrwg.

YOUNG & INEXPERIENCED CYCLISTS

The hills make this ride suitable for families with older children.

REFRESHMENTS

- Cafe at Afan Forest Park.
- Drop Off cafe at Glyncorrwg Mountain Bike Centre.

THINGS TO SEE & DO

- **South Wales Miners' Museum, Cynonville, Afan Forest Park:** museum of the coal-mining industry and its workforce in south Wales; recreation of a tunnel where models of children can be seen crawling through the confined underground space; 01639 851833; www.southwalesminersmuseum.co.uk
- **Afan Forest Park Visitor Centre:** start the popular 'Penhydd' and 'The Wall' mountain bike trails, access the Coed Morgannwg walk, or try a family puzzle trail; 01639 850564; www.afanforestpark.co.uk

A pleasant track in Afan Forest Park

Mountain bikers in
Afan Forest

- Glyncorrwg Ponds & Mountain Bike Centre, Afan Forest Park: activities for everyone, including fishing, canoeing, cycling, walking and, of course, mountain biking; 01639 850564; www.forestry.gov.uk

TRAIN STATIONS
Port Talbot Parkway.

BIKE HIRE
- Skyline Cycles, Afan Forest Park Visitor Centre: 01639 851100; www.skylinecycles.co.uk

FURTHER INFORMATION
- To view or print National Cycle Network routes, visit www.sustrans.org.uk
- Maps for this area are available to buy from www.sustransshop.co.uk
- For further information on routes in Wales, visit www.routes2ride.org.uk/wales
- Neath & Port Talbot Tourist Information: www.visitnpt.co.uk
- Wales Tourist Information: 0870 830 0306; www.visitwales.co.uk

ROUTE DESCRIPTION
Start the ride from Rhyslyn car park in Pontrhydyfen, birthplace of celebrated Welsh actor Richard Burton (1925–84), and follow National Route 885 up the Afan Valley. The route continues on the heavily forested north side of the Afon Afan before continuing north

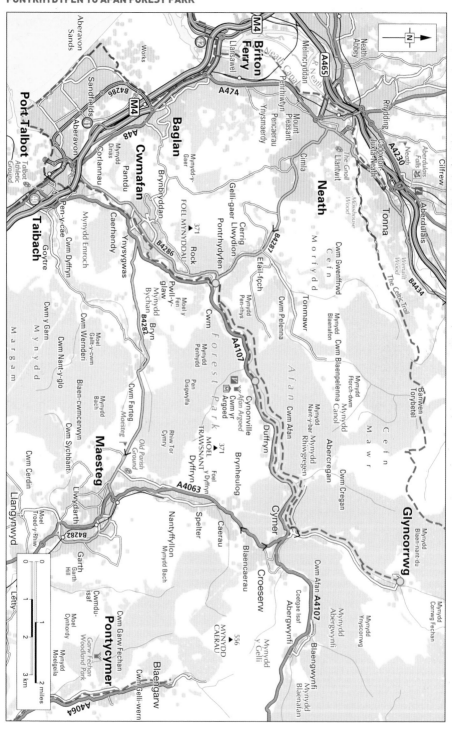

Cycle track bridge over the River Afan

(still alongside the river) to the village of Glyncorrwg, passing the ponds and mountain bike centre en route. From the village, retrace your route for 2 miles (3km) then cross the river on the road bridge at Cymer and pick up the railway path on the south side of the river that leads to the Afan Forest Park Visitor Centre.

At present, the ride starts in Pontrhydyfen because there is just a rough track between Cwmafan and Pontrhydyfen. However, when the Connect2 scheme is completed in 2012/13 there will be an excellent link from Port Talbot Parkway station up past Cwmafan to Pontrhydyfen, which will considerably extend and improve the route.

NEARBY CYCLE ROUTES

Port Talbot is on the Celtic Trail Route (National Route 4), which extends, as a linear trail, for 223 miles (359km) from Fishguard to Chepstow, broadly following the south coast. Route 4, in its entirety, runs between London and Fishguard, via Reading, Bath, Bristol, Newport, Swansea, Carmarthen, Tenby, Haverfordwest and St David's.

There is good family-friendly cycling along the traffic-free trails by the Neath Canal (Route 47) and the Swansea Canal (Route 43).

Mountain bikers of all levels are spoilt for choice with the world-class trails on offer at Afan Forest Park. The Celtic Trail High Level Route option (Route 47) passes to the north of Port Talbot and is joined by Route 4 at Briton Ferry, and also by a link from Glyncorrwg village. Route 47 can be followed east, to Pontypridd, for a challenging and strenuous route that mountain bikers looking for a wild experience will relish.

SWANSEA BIKE PATH

The wide, curving sweep of Swansea Bay is followed on this idyllic cyclepath, which runs from Swansea's delightful Maritime Quarter, along the route of a former railway, to the Victorian seaside town of Mumbles.

The ghost of Dylan Thomas will be your guide. The famous Welsh poet was born in the 'ugly, lovely town', as he described Swansea, and lived there through his formative years. The Dylan Thomas Centre near the start of the route deals comprehensively with the poet's life and works.

As you glide along, you will experience the same splendid panorama of Swansea Bay that Thomas enjoyed as a boy from his bedroom window – a vista that almost certainly influenced his early poems, such as 'The Hill of Sea and Sky is Carried'.

Pedal on to reach Mumbles, once famous for its oyster beds, after which the dramatic 12th-century Oystermouth Castle is named. The castle guarded the landward approach to the Gower and still exudes a formidable presence. Mumbles itself is a picturesque place with a holiday air and lots of choices for eats and drinks. After a break, if you fancy, you can cycle on to Mumbles Head and see the whole of the bay spread out before you.

ROUTE INFORMATION

National Route: 4
Start: Swansea Marina.
Finish: Mumbles Pier.
Distance: 6 miles (9.5km).
Grade: Easy.
Surface: Tarmac.
Hills: None.

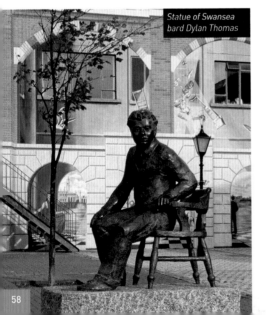

Statue of Swansea bard Dylan Thomas

YOUNG & INEXPERIENCED CYCLISTS

Suitable for families with young children and novices, provided care is taken along unfenced sections by the harbour.

REFRESHMENTS

- Lots of choice in Swansea.
- Junction Box Cafe, near Black Pill.
- Lots of choice in Mumbles.

THINGS TO SEE & DO

- **National Waterfront Museum, Swansea:** learn about the enormous impact of the Industrial Revolution in Wales through historical artefacts and interactive exhibits; 01792 638950; www.museumwales.ac.uk
- **Dylan Thomas Centre, Swansea:** housed in a beautiful building in the Maritime Quarter; permanent exhibition on Dylan Thomas and his life; an annual Dylan Thomas Festival takes place during October and November; 01792 463980; www.swansea.gov.uk
- **Oystermouth Castle, Mumbles:** the Gower's finest castle, standing on a small hill with a magnificent view over Swansea Bay; gloomy passages and haunted dungeons to explore; http://oystermouthcastle.wordpress.com

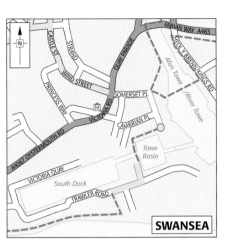

SWANSEA

BIKE HIRE

- Action Bikes, Swansea: 01792 464640
- Schmoos Cycles, Swansea (adult MTB bikes for hire): 01792 467070

FURTHER INFORMATION

- To view or print National Cycle Network routes, visit www.sustrans.org.uk
- Maps for this area are available to buy from www.sustransshop.co.uk
- For further information on routes in Wales, visit www.routes2ride.org.uk/wales
- Swansea Tourist Information: 01792 468321; www.visitswanseabay.com
- Wales Tourist Information: 0870 830 0306; www.visitwales.co.uk

- Gower Coast Adventures, Knab Rock, Mumbles: take a boat trip around the Gower to see razorbills and guillemots nesting on the steep cliffs of Worms Head, grey seals, porpoises and more; 07866 250440; www.gowercoastadventures.co.uk

TRAIN STATIONS

Swansea.

ROUTE DESCRIPTION

From Swansea Marina, follow Route 4 signs (for Llanelli) by the harbour – take care as there are unfenced sections. Cross a footbridge to reach Trawler Road and continue easily along the wide expanse of Swansea Bay, following the line of the old Mumbles Railway. Any kids in your party will probably want to stop here for an ice cream... and who could blame them!

Swansea Maritime Quarter

SWANSEA BIKE PATH

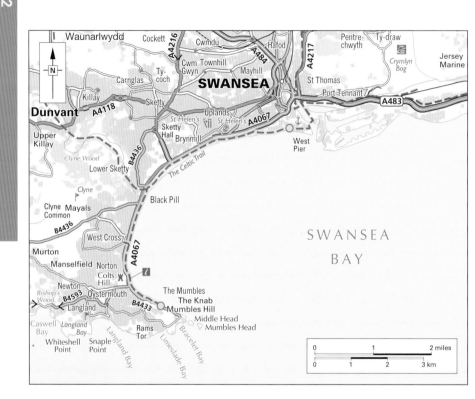

Mumbles Head

Millennium signpost on Swansea Prom

Route 4 follows the deliciously flat cyclepath to Black Pill, where it veers inland on its merry way to Llanelli. The route to the Victorian seaside resort of Mumbles is straight on and soon passes the Junction Box Cafe. Eventually, you reach the outskirts of Mumbles, where you can follow the cyclepath all the way through to Mumbles Pier and perhaps reward yourself with further refreshments.

NEARBY CYCLE ROUTES

The Swansea Marina to Mumbles trail is part of the longer Celtic Trail (National Route 4), which it follows along Swansea Bay to Black Pill, where Route 4 leads inland. In its entirety, this route extends across Wales, crossing the country's widest point and broadly following the south coast from Chepstow in the east to Fishguard. The many traffic-free sections are ideal for family cycling.

Route 43 leads up the River Tawe from the centre of Swansea along an excellent 13-mile (21km) traffic-free section to Ystalyfera (near Ystradgynlais), via Pontardawe. Between Clydach and Pontardawe, there is a 5-mile (8km) section alongside the only remaining water-filled part of the Swansea Canal. Route 43 is being developed further north and will ultimately connect Swansea with Builth Wells, via the Swansea Valley (Tawe Valley) and the Brecon Beacons National Park.

Route 47 – the Celtic Trail High Level Route option – can be joined east of Swansea at Briton Ferry. From there, the initial section, along the Neath Canal, is a great traffic-free, family-friendly ride, which can be followed to Tonna.

MILLENNIUM COASTAL PARK – KIDWELLY TO LLANELLI

Kidwelly is a town dominated by the massive towers of its castle, which is still in remarkably good condition. The town and castle were built by the Normans in the 12th century. Below the castle walls a bridge dating back to the 14th century spans the Gwendraeth Fach River. The 13th-century Gothic church once served as a Benedictine monastery. Kidwelly prospered during the Industrial Revolution and was the location of a large brickworks and tinworks, the history of which can be explored further in the town's Industrial Museum.

The Millennium Coastal Park/Parc Arfordirol Y Mileniwm was originally a project started by Llanelli Borough Council to turn a 12-mile (19.5km) stretch of industrial wasteland along the coast into a green recreational corridor. It is now one of the most popular sections of the National Cycle Network in Wales, offering superb views across the Loughor Estuary to the hills of the Gower peninsula. There is a series of attractions along the route, including Pembrey Country Park, which backs onto the long sandy beach of Cefn Sidan; the newly created marina at Burry Port; Sandy Water Park (with an option to explore the trail up Swiss Valley); the Discovery Centre at Llanelli's North Dock; and the National Wetlands Centre at Llwynhendy.

Kidwelly Castle

ROUTE INFORMATION
National Route: 4
Start: Banc Pen-dre, Kidwelly town centre.
Finish: Bynea train station.
Distance: 18 miles (29km). Shorter options: Kidwelly to Pembrey Country Park 6 miles (9.5km); Burry Port to Pembrey Country Park 3.5 miles (5.5km); Penclacwydd to Llanelli 4.5 miles (7km); Penclacwydd to Burry Port 7 miles (11km).
Grade: Easy.
Surface: Mixture of tarmac and gravel paths.
Hills: None.

YOUNG & INEXPERIENCED CYCLISTS
There is a short on-road section at the start in Kidwelly, where care should be taken. This is an excellent route for young children, provided you take account of the wind!

REFRESHMENTS

- Lots of choice in Kidwelly, Burry Port and Llanelli.
- Cafe at Pembrey Country Park.
- Cafe at Discovery Centre in the Millennium Coastal Park, near Llanelli.
- Cafe at the National Wetland Centre in Penclacwydd at the end of the ride.

THINGS TO SEE & DO

- **Kidwelly Industrial Museum:** 01554 891078; www.kidwellyindustrialmuseum.co.uk
- **Kidwelly Castle:** impressive remains dating back to the 12th century; 01554 890104; http://cadw.wales.gov.uk

- **Pembrey Country Park:** attractions include a dry ski slope, 9-hole pitch and putt course, miniature railway, large adventure playground, cafe and an 8-mile (13km) long beach; 01554 833913; www.onebiggarden.com
- **Views of Gower Peninsula:** spectacular coastline and the first place in Britain designated an Area of Outstanding Natural Beauty (AONB).
- **Discovery Centre:** located in the heart of the Millennium Coastal Park, with an information centre, children's play area, exhibitions and refreshments; 01554 777744; www.onebiggarden.com

Burry Port lighthouse

MILLENNIUM COASTAL PARK
KIDWELLY TO LLANELLI

FURTHER INFORMATION
- To view or print National Cycle Network routes, visit www.sustrans.org.uk
- Maps for this area are available to buy from www.sustransshop.co.uk
- For more information on routes in Wales, visit www.routes2ride.org.uk/wales
- Carmarthenshire Tourist Information: www.discovercarmarthenshire.com
- Wales Tourist Information: 0870 830 0306; www.visitwales.co.uk

ROUTE DESCRIPTION
Starting from Kidwelly, you quickly join a traffic-free path that continues more or less unbroken to Bynea, to the east of Llanelli. You soon enter the sandy woodlands of Pembrey Forest, where there are many cycle tracks based around the visitor centre.

Beyond Pembrey Forest, the route follows long sections of cyclepaths with wonderful views. Between Burry Port and Llanelli, you cross the railway line twice via huge land bridges covered with earth and grass.

Towards the end of the ride, you could visit the National Wetland Centre in Llanelli before continuing on to Bynea, where you can catch a train back to Kidwelly via Llanelli, though services are limited from this station. Alternatively, you can press on to Swansea, from where there are regular train services.

- National Wetland Centre Wales, Llanelli: includes the Millennium Wetland complex, home to wildlife as diverse as dragonflies and little egrets; 01554 741087; www.wwt.org.uk

TRAIN STATIONS
Kidwelly; Burry Port; Llanelli; Bynea.

BIKE HIRE
- Pembrey Country Park: 01554 834443
- Merlin Cycles: Discovery Centre, North Dock, Llanelli: 01554 756603

NEARBY CYCLE ROUTES
The ride described here is part of National Route 4, the Celtic Trail/Lôn Geltaidd, which runs from Fishguard to the old Severn Bridge near Chepstow.

National Route 47 runs north from Llanelli via Swiss Valley to Cross Hands, with a 14-mile (22.5km) traffic-free section (see page 66).

National Route 43 will eventually link Swansea to Builth Wells, where it joins Lôn Las Cymru from Cardiff to Anglesey (National Route 8).

There are many more tracks to explore in Pembrey Forest, around the Country Park.

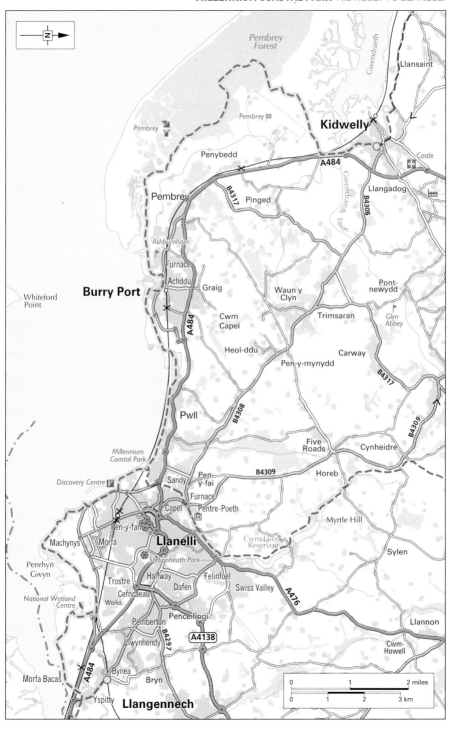

SWISS VALLEY CYCLE ROUTE – LLANELLI TO CROSS HANDS

This traffic-free route is a joy to cycle, following a disused railway line up to a picturesque double reservoir set among hills.

The route starts easily from the sail-shaped Discovery Centre at the Millennium Coastal Park in the seaside town of Llanelli and leads to Sandy Water Park, a successfully reclaimed steelworks site. From here, the Swiss Valley Route climbs into the rolling hills above Llanelli, passing the hallowed Stradey Park rugby ground and through the hop-infused air by the Felinfoel Brewery.

This long-established brewery had humble beginnings. Its founder, David John, bought the King's Head pub in the 1830s but, unfortunately for him, this popular coaching inn was adjacent to a toll gate. At the time, hard-pressed tenant farmers, known as the Rebecca rioters, were on the rampage, moving through Carmarthenshire and destroying toll gates. The king wasn't a popular monarch, so David John wisely renamed his tavern the Union Inn, and his own-brewed beers soon became popular. Today, Felinfoel beers are sold throughout the UK, with Double Dragon a firm favourite.

ROUTE INFORMATION
National Routes: 47, 4
Start: Discovery Centre at North Dock, Llanelli.
Finish: Near the cinema in Cross Hands.
Distance: 13 miles (21km).
Grade: Moderate.
Surface: Tarmac.
Hills: Gradual incline.

YOUNG & INEXPERIENCED CYCLISTS
Ideal for young families and novices.

REFRESHMENTS
- The Estuary Cafe, National Wetland Centre, Llanelli.
- Flanagan's Coastline Cafe, Discovery Centre, Llanelli.
- The Mediterranean Cafe and Seasons Restaurant, National Botanic Garden of Wales, Llanarthney.

THINGS TO SEE & DO
- National Wetland Centre Wales, Llanelli: stretching over almost 450 acres on the Burry Inlet; an important home to species as diverse as dragonflies and little egrets; interactive Millennium Discovery Centre and Water Vole City; 01554 741087;

www.wwt.org.uk
- Discovery Centre, Llanelli: overlooks Llanelli beach, with panoramic views of the Loughor Estuary and the Gower; offers visitors an excellent introduction to the wildlife-rich Millennium Coastal Park; 01554 777744; www.onebiggarden.com
- Lliedi Reservoirs, Swiss Valley: the Swiss Valley Cycle Route runs right by these two upland reservoirs; the lower of the two in particular makes an ideal picnic spot.
- National Botanic Garden of Wales,

This route offers green and pleasant cycling

Llanarthney: 5 miles (8km) northwest of Cross Hands; visionary project and botanical science showcase built for the Millennium; 01558 668768; www.gardenofwales.org.uk

TRAIN STATIONS
Llanelli.

BIKE HIRE
- Merlin Cycles, Discovery Centre, Llanelli: 01554 756603

FURTHER INFORMATION
- To view or print National Cycle Network routes, visit www.sustrans.org.uk

SWISS VALLEY CYCLE ROUTE

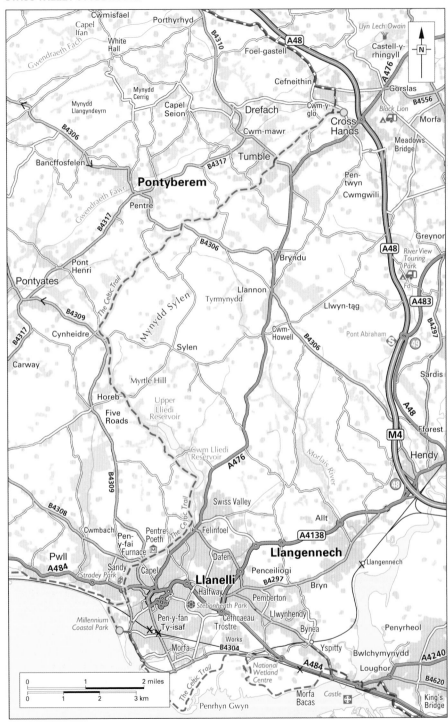

Gorgeous views along the way

Wildlife in the Millennium Coastal Park

- Maps for this area are available to buy from www.sustransshop.co.uk
- For further information on routes in Wales, visit www.routes2ride.org.uk/wales
- **Carmarthen Tourist Information:** 01267 231557; www.visit.carmarthenshire.gov.uk
- **Llanelli Tourist Information:** 01554 777744; www.onebiggarden.com
- **Wales Tourist Information:** 0870 830 0306; www.visitwales.co.uk

ROUTE DESCRIPTION

From the Discovery Centre at North Dock, Llanelli, follow the old railway line and signs for Route 47. There is a gentle 168m (550ft) climb up from the town. Further on, the route sidles by the Cwm Lliedi and Upper Lliedi Reservoirs. Here, you can enjoy some peace, with good views over the Gwendraeth Valley. From there, continue easily to the finish point at the cinema in Cross Hands. If you return to Llanelli on Route 47, you can enjoy a gravity-aided journey.

NEARBY CYCLE ROUTES

Llanelli is a great starting point for exploring traffic-free trails on the National Cycle Network in south Wales, as it acts as a hub for several routes. It lies at a halfway point in the magnificent Millennium Coastal Park, with trails running west towards Pembrey Country Park (see page 62), and east towards Swansea.

The Swiss Valley Route is part of the High Level Route option on the Celtic Trail, which runs from Fishguard to Chepstow. This long-distance route crosses Wales at its widest point, on an inland route, and is packed with interest throughout its length.

The Swiss Valley Route also links with the more coast-orientated Celtic Trail Low Level Route (Route 4) at the Discovery Centre at Llanelli. This can be followed from Llanelli to Fishguard, via Tenby. Route 4, in its entirety, runs between London and Fishguard, via Reading, Bath, Bristol, Newport, Swansea, Carmarthen, Tenby, Haverfordwest and St David's.

BRUNEL TRAIL

Neyland was no more than a small fishing village until 1856, when Isambard Kingdom Brunel decided it should become the western terminus of his Great Western Railway, bringing passengers from London to ships bound for southern Ireland or even across the Atlantic.

The passenger trade ceased at the end of the 19th century but Neyland continued to flourish as a fishing port until 1964, when operations closed down. The economic decline that followed was halted in the late 1980s with the building of the new marina. The Cleddau Bridge, a crucial road link between the south and north banks of the waterway, opened in 1975, replacing the ferry that used to run between Neyland and Hobbs Point.

The Brunel Trail/Llwybr Brunel climbs along the old railway path, linking Neyland Marina with Haverfordwest, the headquarters of the county and the market town for most of Pembrokeshire, with its important location at the tidal limit of the Western Cleddau River.

ROUTE INFORMATION

National Route: 4
Start: Pembroke Dock train station or Brunel Quay, Neyland Marina, near Pembroke.
Finish: Haverfordwest train station.

Distance: 9 miles (14.5km) from Brunel Quay; 11 miles (17.5km) from Pembroke Dock station
Grade: Easy.
Surface: Tarmac or gravel.

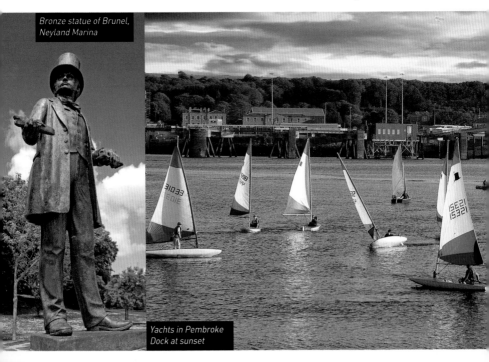

Bronze statue of Brunel, Neyland Marina

Yachts in Pembroke Dock at sunset

Hills: Some short climbs; moderate gradients.

YOUNG & INEXPERIENCED CYCLISTS
Traffic-free. One busy road on the approach to Neyland and a few minor roads to cross.

REFRESHMENTS
- Cafe at Brunel Quay.
- Choices in Neyland.
- Lots of choice in Haverfordwest.

THINGS TO SEE & DO
- Westfield Pill Nature Reserve.
- Cleddau Estuary.
- **Neyland Marina:** picturesque and sheltered yachting marina.
- **Haverfordwest Priory:** recently excavated remains of an early 13th-century Augustinian priory, with the only surviving ecclesiastical medieval garden in Britain; http://cadw.wales.gov.uk
- **Haverfordwest Castle:** founded by Gilbert de Clare in the early 12th century; 01437 763087; www.haverfordwest-town-museum.org.uk
- **Haverfordwest Town Museum:** open Easter to October; 01437 763087; www.haverfordwest-town-museum.org.uk

TRAIN STATIONS
Pembroke Dock; Johnston; Haverfordwest.

BIKE HIRE
- **Mike's Bikes, Haverfordwest:** 01437 760068; www.mikes-bikes.co.uk

FURTHER INFORMATION
- To view or print National Cycle Network routes, visit www.sustrans.org.uk
- Maps for this area are available to buy from www.sustransshop.co.uk
- For more information on routes in Wales,

HAVERFORDWEST

BRUNEL TRAIL

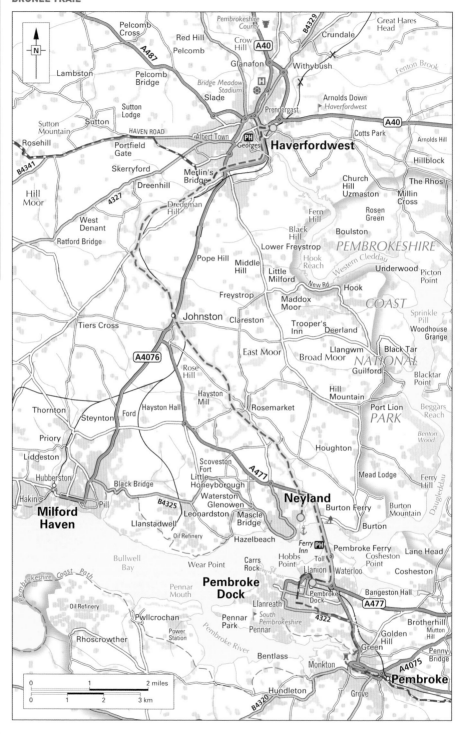

The atmospheric ruins of Haverfordwest Priory

visit www.routes2ride.org.uk/wales
- **Haverfordwest Tourist Information:** 01437 763110; www.visitpembrokeshire.com
- **Wales Tourist Information:** 0870 830 0306; www.visitwales.co.uk

ROUTE DESCRIPTION

From Pembroke Dock train station, follow National Route 4 signs over the Cleddau Bridge. Either cycle to Honeyborough Roundabout, then turn left off the route onto the road into Neyland, or follow signs after the second bridge, which involves crossing the busy road, then heading down a very steep shale footpath alongside the bridge and into Westfield Pill.

At Neyland, the route starts at Brunel Quay, and initially shares a traffic-calmed road through the marina before linking up with a path through Westfield Pill Nature Reserve, where you may need to dismount to get through the A-frame barriers. There is car parking available at the marina, and a cafe serving meals and hot drinks – you might want to make the most of this opportunity for refreshments, as there is only a small shop in Johnston.

Once you reach the railway path, the route is self-contained, mostly tarmac and well signposted. The route crosses three narrow lanes, which are clearly visible and without much traffic. The route rises gently from Neyland to Johnston through woodland and farmland. At Johnston, the route continues north to Haverfordwest, via a purpose-built wooden cycleway alongside the existing railway line. Leave Route 4 at Merlin's Bridge and follow the cycle lanes into Haverfordwest town centre and to the train station, or continue on Route 4 on-road to Broad Haven and then north to St David's, enjoying the stunning views of the Pembrokeshire coastline.

NEARBY CYCLE ROUTES

The Brunel Trail is part of National Route 4 and the Celtic Trail, which goes from Chepstow to Fishguard via Swansea.

WELSH WILDLIFE CENTRE TO CENARTH FALLS

This is a route full of variety and places of unique interest. Along Lôn Teifi (National Route 82), the ride closely follows the River Teifi – one of the most important salmon rivers in Wales. You'll love it.

It all starts with a bang at the Welsh Wildlife Centre to the north of Cilgerran, with panoramic views over the River Teifi, Cardigan town and woodland. The Teifi Marshes Nature Reserve on the banks of the river is home to otters, beautiful kingfishers and brightly coloured dragonflies. The centre also has an adventure playground, with lots of slides and living willow structures.

Beyond Cilgerran, the castle (with the same name) is a highlight, sitting on a rocky promontory above the river. Despite its position, this castle may have been the scene of the abduction of a beauty named Nest in 1109. However, Nest wasn't too put out and went on to have a number of lovers, including King Henry I, earning herself notoriety as the 'Helen of Wales'.

Sitting by the end of the route, at Cenarth Falls, you can laze about and watch for jumping salmon. You might even spot some strange craft on the water – the remarkable Coracle Centre is located here, set in the grounds of a 17th-century flour mill beside a 200-year-old bridge.

ROUTE INFORMATION
National Route: 82
Start: Welsh Wildlife Centre, Cilgerran.
Finish: Cenarth Falls.
Distance: 9 miles (14.5km).
Grade: Moderate.
Surface: Tarmac.
Hills: The route is undulating, with some short climbs; the longest is where the route joins the B4332 by Abercych.

YOUNG & INEXPERIENCED CYCLISTS
Most of the route is on quiet roads, although there is a busier section – the B4332 – for the final 2 miles (3km).

REFRESHMENTS
• Options in Cilgerran, Abercych and Cenarth.

THINGS TO SEE & DO
• Welsh Wildlife Centre, Cilgerran: informative interactive indoor display of local natural and social history; interactive screens with live camera feeds from the Teifi Marshes Nature Reserve;

01239 621600; www.welshwildlife.org
• Heritage Canoes, near the Welsh Wildlife Centre, Cilgerran: experienced guides will tell you the story of the Teifi Gorge and help you identify the wildlife as you follow the river to Cilgerran Castle; 01239 613961; www.cardiganbayactive.co.uk
• Cilgerran Castle: striking 13th-century ruined castle, with earlier Norman origins

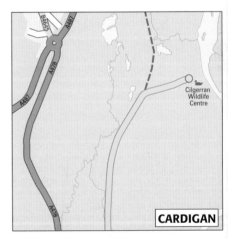

CARDIGAN

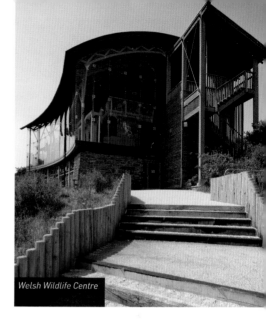

and boasting two impressive and highly defensible round towers; overlooks the spectacular Teifi Gorge; 01239 621339; www.nationaltrust.org.uk

- National Coracle Centre, Cenarth Falls: fascinating museum of coracles from across the world and a workshop; includes a section on the implements and methods used in poaching; 01239 710980; www.coraclemuseum.co.uk

TRAIN STATIONS
None.

BIKE HIRE
- New Image Bicycles, Cardigan: 01239 621275; www.newimagebicycles.co.uk

FURTHER INFORMATION
- To view or print National Cycle Network routes, visit www.sustrans.org.uk
- Maps for this area are available to buy from www.sustransshop.co.uk
- For further information on routes in Wales, visit www.routes2ride.org.uk/wales

Welsh Wildlife Centre

- Mid Wales Tourist Information: 01654 702653; www.visitmidwales.co.uk
- Wales Tourist Information: 0870 830 0306; www.visitwales.co.uk

ROUTE DESCRIPTION
The route is quite easy to follow and should be well signed throughout. From the Welsh Wildlife Centre near Cilgerran, follow Route 82

Coracle race on the River Teifi

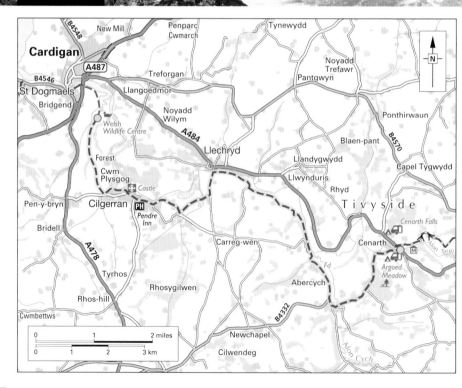

Cenarth Falls

into the village itself. The route follows a back road through Cilgerran before joining the main road further on. Continue east to Cilgerran Castle, set in an enchanting location overlooking the Teifi Gorge.

A thrilling downhill ride leads to a tight bend, where the route swings to the left. Thereafter, it follows a network of quiet and minor roads by the River Teifi. Cycle on through Abercych, after which Lôn Teifi joins the B4332 for the final run to Cenarth. There is, unfortunately, an initial climb, but after that you can coast down to Cenarth Falls and enjoy a well-earned rest.

Cilgerran Castle ruins

NEARBY CYCLE ROUTES

The Welsh Wildlife Centre to Cenarth Falls trail is part of the longer Lôn Teifi (National Route 82), which runs between Aberystwyth and Fishguard.

Lôn Teifi is a 98-mile (158km) cycle route that follows country lanes and minor roads along the valley of the River Teifi. It connects the rural towns of Tregaron, Lampeter, Llandysul and Newcastle Emlyn, before

continuing to Cardigan, 3 miles (5km) downstream from Cilgerran.

Lôn Cambria (Route 81) links with Route 82 to the south of Aberystwyth, at Pontrhydygroes. Lôn Cambria crosses the heart of mid-Wales between Aberystwyth and Shrewsbury. The 113-mile (182km) ride leads along a pleasant mixture of river valleys, trails, mountain roads and country lanes, giving fine views of the countryside along the way.

LLANGOLLEN TO PONTCYSYLLTE AQUEDUCT

The lovely town of Llangollen is the gateway to north Wales. The area is rich with mountains, white water rivers including the spectacular River Dee, canals with horse-drawn boats, as well as the Llangollen Railway with steam trains that chug along the Dee Valley, the Horseshoe Pass and the Horseshoe Falls. Famous and historic buildings grace the town, including Plas Newydd, home to the 'Ladies of Llangollen' and the Royal Pavilion, host to year-round events including the International Eisteddfod.

In 2009, the 11-mile (17.5km) section of the Llangollen Canal from Gledrid Bridge near Rhoswiel through to the Horseshoe Falls, which includes Pontcysyllte Aqueduct, was designated a UNESCO World Heritage Site. Pontcysyllte is the highest and longest aqueduct on the UK canal system and was built by Thomas Telford 200 years ago. You can cross it on foot or by boat from the Wharf in Llangollen and marvel at Telford's feat of engineering. You can also take a horse-drawn boat to the canal's source.

The Llangollen Canal

LLANGOLLEN TO PONTCYSYLLTE AQUEDUCT

ROUTE INFORMATION
National Route: 85
Start: Llangollen Wharf.
Finish: Pontcysyllte Aqueduct at Trevor.
Distance: 5 miles (8km).
Grade: Easy.
Surface: Tarmac and dust paths.
Hills: Mainly flat.

YOUNG & INEXPERIENCED CYCLISTS
The route is traffic-free and perfect for young
and inexperienced riders.

13th-century Valle
Crucis Abbey ruins

Pontcysyllte Aqueduct

REFRESHMENTS
- Llangollen Wharf cafe.
- Plenty of choice in Llangollen.
- Sun Inn, Trevor Uchaf.
- Bryn Howell Hotel.
- Basic refreshments at Trevor Basin.

THINGS TO SEE & DO
- **Llangollen Horse Drawn Boats:** 01978 860702; www.horsedrawnboats.co.uk
- **Llangollen Heritage Railway:** www.llangollen-railway.co.uk
- **Plas Newydd:** elegant house on the shores of the Menai Strait; 01978 861314; www.llangollen.com/plas.html
- **Dinas Bran Castle:** ruins of a once-great castle, with spectacular views; www.llangollen.com/castle.html
- **Valle Crucis Abbey:** once home to Cistercian monks; www.llangollen.com/valle.html
- **Pontcysyllte Aqueduct:** the longest and highest cast-iron aqueduct in the world www.llangollen.org

TRAIN STATIONS
Ruabon; Chirk.

BIKE HIRE
- **ProAdventure:** 01978 861912; www.proadventure.co.uk

FURTHER INFORMATION
- To view or print National Cycle Network routes, visit www.sustrans.org.uk
- Maps for this area are available to buy from www.sustransshop.co.uk
- For more information on routes in Wales, visit www.routes2ride.org.uk/wales
- **Wales Tourist Information:** 0870 830 0306; www.visitwales.co.uk

ROUTE DESCRIPTION
On leaving the canal wharf, head eastwards out of town past the canal boat moorings – please take care along this narrow section. It's easy to follow this route as you stay on the towpath for the whole 5 miles (8km). After 2 miles (3km) you can take a steep detour up through Trevor Uchaf to the wonderful Trevor Rocks area, sometimes known as the Panorama for its excellent views.

Continue eastwards on the canal and just before you reach the Bryn Howel Hotel you will pass under the disused railway bridge that used to carry the Ruabon to Barmouth railway line. At the eastern end the route leads you into Trevor Basin, where canal boats are moored or preparing themselves to cross the world-famous aqueduct. Make sure you take a walk across it yourself!

NEARBY CYCLE ROUTES
You can ride from the southern side of the aqueduct to Chirk alongside the canal but please note that not all of the towpath has been improved to the standard of the Llangollen to Pontcysyllte section, although plans to upgrade it in the next couple of years are under way. There are also lots of mountain biking opportunities in the local area.

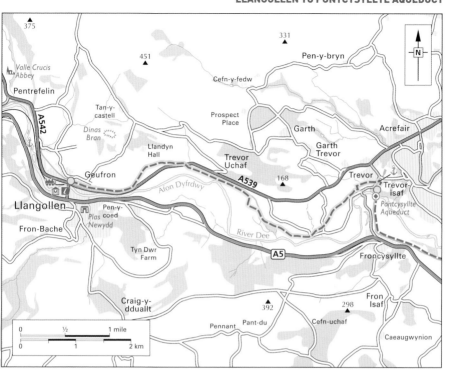

Pontcysyllte
Aqueduct

YSTWYTH TRAIL – ABERYSTWYTH TO TREGARON

The recently opened Ystwyth Trail (Llwybr Ystwyth) leads through the attractive Ceredigion countryside and has something to appeal to every level of cyclist. It follows the line of the Great Western Railway, which came to Aberystwyth in 1867.

Aberystwyth, a fishing town, grew with the advent of the railway. Nowadays, this old line provides a fine path for those on two wheels and even horseback. As well as following the tranquil Ystwyth Valley, the route crosses the Cors Caron National Nature Reserve. This wildlife haven is one of the finest raised bog systems in Britain, formed from the compression of millions and millions of mosses. Peat was traditionally cut here but now the area is recognized for its ecological importance and unique flora. Red kites can also be seen on the reserve. During the winter months (at 2pm), you can watch these beautiful, once-persecuted birds being fed from the road bridge on the A485 (Tregaron to Aberystwyth road), about 1 mile (1.6km) outside Tregaron.

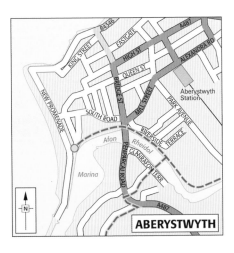

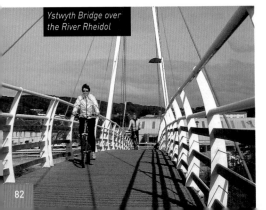

Ystwyth Bridge over the River Rheidol

ROUTE INFORMATION

National Routes: 81, 82, 820
Start: Aberystwyth Marina.
Finish: Tregaron.
Distance: 20 miles (32km).
Grade: Easy to moderate.
Surface: Gravel and tarmac.
Hills: Mainly level as far as Felin Dyffryn. Two significant hills between Trawscoed (Crosswood) and Tynygraig, followed by a steep descent. Then it's mainly level to Tregaron.

YOUNG & INEXPERIENCED CYCLISTS

The traffic-free sections of the trail (see route description) are ideal for families with young children and novices. The complete trail is suitable only for experienced cyclists.

REFRESHMENTS

- Lots of choice in Aberystwyth.
- Various options in Llanilar and Tregaron.

THINGS TO SEE & DO

- Aberystwyth Castle: 13th-century castle, with superb views over the Irish Sea; previously an important seat of Welsh government; 01970 612125; www.visitmidwales.co.uk

Steam train on the Rheidol Railway

- **Vale of Rheidol Railway, near Aberystwyth:** once a working link between local lead mines and the harbour; now runs steam trains for visitors through the Rheidol Valley; 01970 625819; www.rheidolrailway.co.uk
- **Cors Caron National Nature Reserve, Tregaron:** one of the finest raised bog systems in Britain; sundews, bog rosemary and cotton grasses thrive; http://countryside.wales.info
- **The Kite Centre & Museum, Tregaron:** learn about the local red kite population and recent sightings on Cors Caron Nature Reserve and the old railway line to Tregaron; 01974 298977

TRAIN STATIONS
Aberystwyth.

BIKE HIRE
- **On Your Bike, Aberystwyth:** 01970 626996

FURTHER INFORMATION
- To view or print National Cycle Network routes, visit www.sustrans.org.uk
- Maps for this area are available to buy from www.sustransshop.co.uk
- Free leaflet and information from www.ystwythtrail.org.uk
- For further information on routes in Wales, visit www.routes2ride.org.uk/wales
- **Aberystwyth Tourist Information:** 01970 612125; www.visitmidwales.co.uk
- **Wales Tourist Information:** 0870 830 0306; www.visitwales.co.uk

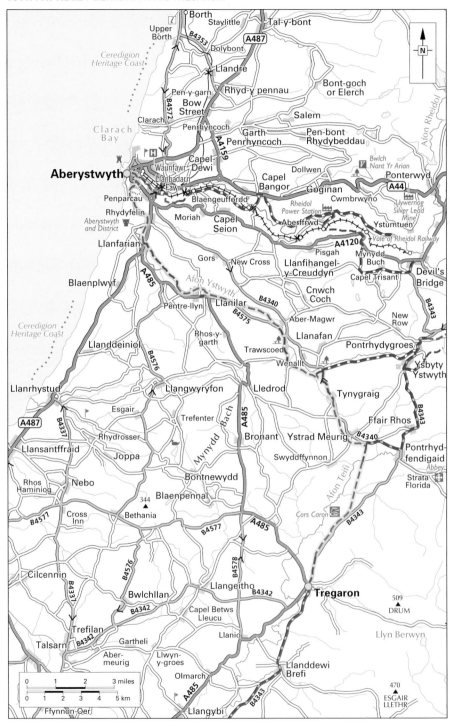

The magnificent red kite

ROUTE DESCRIPTION

From Aberystwyth Marina, follow signs for Routes 81 and 82 and cross the River Rheidol on a new bridge. On the far side, follow signs and the cyclepath that runs pleasantly by the River Ystwyth.

Meet the A487 to the north of Llanfarian, and cross it with care. Follow the route ahead on a minor road, rejoin the old railway trackbed, and follow it up the Ystwyth Valley. Meet the B4575 to the north of Trawscoed (Crosswood), then climb steeply on a minor road. By Dolfor, rejoin a section of cyclepath leading briefly onto the B4340 before rejoining the railway for a traffic-free section to Ystrad Meurig. The remainder of the route follows quiet cyclepaths and busier on-road sections.

NEARBY CYCLE ROUTES

The Ystwyth Trail is part of the longer National Route 82, which runs between Aberystwyth and Fishguard. Much of its length is known as Lôn Teifi – a 98-mile (158km) cycle route on country lanes and minor roads along the valley of the River Teifi. Lôn Teifi connects the rural towns of Tregaron, Lampeter, Llandysul and Newcastle Emlyn before reaching Cardigan.

Route 81 (Lôn Cambria) also begins in Aberystwyth. Crossing the heart of mid-Wales between Aberystwyth and Shrewsbury, this 113-mile (182km) ride leads along river valleys, trails, mountain roads and country lanes, giving fine views of the countryside along the way. It links with Lôn Teifi at Pontrhydygroes, to the south of Aberystwyth.

Experienced cyclists could follow minor roads and the B4343 from Route 81, near Pontrhydygroes, to join the Rheidol Trail.

ELAN VALLEY TRAIL

The Elan Valley reservoirs were built in the early 20th century to supply the growing city of Birmingham with water. Until then, many of the city's inhabitants drew their water from polluted wells, and this, combined with the crowded and unsanitary conditions in the slum districts, often led to epidemics of typhoid and cholera. With the building of the new dams and reservoirs, clean, fresh water was carried from mid-Wales to Birmingham via a 73-mile (117km) pipeline.

The reservoirs are truly spectacular, set among the mountains of mid-Wales, surrounded by mixed woodland and boasting some of the most beautiful dams in the whole of the country. The Elan Valley Trail/Llwybr Cwm Elan follows the line of the old Birmingham Corporation Railway, which was used to carry materials for building the dams. At the dam at the southern end of Craig Goch Reservoir, you will probably choose to turn around and head downhill back to Rhayader. However, if you are feeling fit, you could complete a challenging loop by following the lane north, then dropping back to Rhayader via the Aberystwyth Mountain Road. The trail forms part of Lôn Cambria (National Route 81), which runs east from Aberystwyth through Rhayader to Shrewsbury.

ROUTE INFORMATION
National Routes: 81, 8
Start: West side of Rhayader.
Finish: Craig Goch Reservoir.
Distance: 9 miles (14.5km).
Grade: Moderate.
Surface: Tarmac or gravel.

A pleasant day's fishing in the Elan Valley

Hills: There is a gradual climb up to Elan Valley Visitor Centre, but this makes an excellent descent on the return journey.

YOUNG & INEXPERIENCED CYCLISTS
The ride is essentially traffic-free along an old railway line, although there are a few short on-road sections.

REFRESHMENTS
- Lots of choice in Rhayader.
- Cafe at Elan Valley Visitor Centre.

THINGS TO SEE & DO
- Elan Valley reservoirs and visitor centre: learn more about the construction of the reservoirs; seasonal opening times; 01597 810880; www.elanvalley.org.uk
- Carngafallt, Elan Village: RSPB nature reserve, where you can see a wide variety of birds and possibly badgers and hares as well; 01654 700222; www.rspb.org.uk

TRAIN STATIONS
Llandrindod Wells. It is 15 miles (24km) from Llandrindod Wells to the route start at Rhayader. If you want to hire a bike, you can

use the bus service from Llandrindod Wells to Rhayader. If you want to arrive by train with your bike, you can follow the Radnor Ring on-road from the station to Newbridge-on-Wye and then pick up National Route 8 northwards to Rhayader (about 13.5 miles/22km).

BIKE HIRE

- Clive Powell Mountain Bike Centre, Rhayader: 01597 811343; www.clivepowell-mtb.co.uk

FURTHER INFORMATION

- To view or print National Cycle Network routes, visit www.sustrans.org.uk
- Maps for this area are available to buy from www.sustransshop.co.uk
- For more information on routes in Wales, visit www.routes2ride.org.uk/wales
- **Wales Tourist Information:** 0870 830 0306; www.visitwales.co.uk

ROUTE DESCRIPTION

National Route 81, to the west of Rhayader, follows the former trackbed of the railway built

Cycling along beside Lower Elan Reservoir

by the Birmingham Corporation to carry materials and workers for building the reservoir system at the turn of the 20th century. The project was conducted with unusual sensitivity: the Elan Valley has retained some wildness and natural beauty, and the reservoirs resemble natural lakes.

The stylish gateway to the railway path marks the beginning of your ride through this

The Foel valve tower on the Garreg-Ddu Reservoir

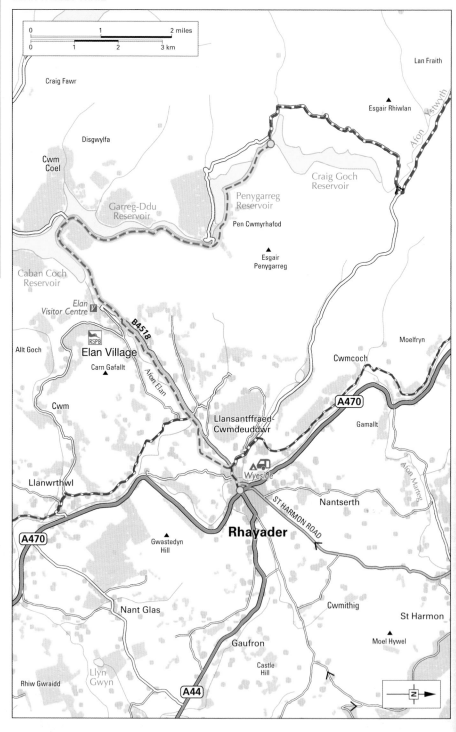

beautiful wooded valley. The visitor centre (with toilets, information, cafe and play area) is halfway up the trail, making it an ideal resting place, although there is a long descent to the visitor centre from the main trail. Ride along the north bank of Caban Coch Reservoir and then up the eastern edge of Garreg-Ddu and Penygarreg Reservoirs. The beauty of this ride is the landscape, with waterfalls tumbling down hills topped by ancient cairns.

The trail ends at the car park at the southern end of Craig Goch Reservoir, where there are also toilets. National Route 81 continues northwards on-road towards Aberystwyth. To get back to Rhayader, turn around and retrace your outward route. Alternatively, if you're on a mountain bike, you have the option of heading north on a (hilly) bridleway via a Roman camp to the lane that will take you back into Rhayader.

Scenic cycling by the Lower Elan Reservoir

NEARBY CYCLE ROUTES
National Route 8, known as Lôn Las Cymru, which links Holyhead to Cardiff, runs through Rhayader and uses a section of the Elan Trail.

Regional Route 25, known as the Radnor Ring, is a delightful circular ride linking Rhayader with Llandrindod Wells. There are other quiet lanes and bridleways around Rhayader, which make it such an ideal base for a weekend's cycling.

Mid-Wales also has a number of Wales Cycle Breaks Centres at Rhayader, Knighton/Presteigne and Brecon. Visit www.cyclebreakswales.com or www.gwyliaubeiciocymru.com for further details.

Waterfall by Penygarreg Reservoir

INSTANT CANAL KARMA – NEWTOWN TO ABERMULE

Newtown (Y Drenewydd) sits by the banks of the River Severn and is the largest town in mid-Wales. It's famous as the birthplace in 1771 of the social reformer Robert Owen, who became one of Britain's first advocates of improved conditions for workers, setting up a model cotton mill at New Lanark in Scotland.

The route, which is traffic-free throughout, is ideal for families and follows a scenic section by the River Severn and the Montgomery Canal (known locally as 'The Monty'). From Newtown to Aberbechan, it runs along a newly opened cyclepath and from there follows a subsequent segment, by the canal and Severn, to Abermule.

Unlike the vast majority of those built in Wales to serve the coalfields, mines and industrial areas, this canal was constructed to transport lime, used to improve the soil of the Upper Severn Valley. Today, the canal is a declared Site of Special Scientific Interest (SSSI) for over two-thirds of its length – it is one of the most important sites in the world for floating water plantain, and wildlife thrives along its banks.

In Abermule, you can enjoy refreshments in the welcoming Abermule Hotel. Originally the Railway Hotel, it was renamed after a tragic accident, known as the 'Great Abermule Train Disaster', on 26 January 1921, which resulted in the death of 17 passengers, including the Cambrian Railways chairman.

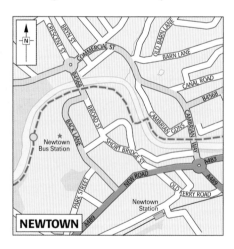

ROUTE INFORMATION
National Route: 81
Start: Riverside, near Newtown bus station.
Finish: Abermule.
Distance: 5 miles (8km).
Grade: Easy.
Surface: Tarmac and gravel.
Hills: Mainly flat.

YOUNG & INEXPERIENCED CYCLISTS
This route is ideal for families with young children and novices.

REFRESHMENTS
- Lots of choice in Newtown.
- Abermule Hotel and other choices in Abermule.

THINGS TO SEE & DO
- **Robert Owen Museum, Newtown:** the only museum dedicated solely to Robert Owen, the 18th-century visionary socialist and father of the Co-operative Movement; 01686 627901; www.robert-owen-museum.org.uk
- **Newtown Textile Museum:** open June to August; housed in a fine example of an early 19th-century weaving shop; learn about the people who would have operated the hand looms; 01686 622024; www.powys.gov.uk
- **Pwll Penarth Nature Reserve, near Llanllwchaiarn:** bird paradise on the site of a former sewage works; two hides ensure

Newtown and the
River Severn

Bronze statue of
Robert Owen

good views over a lake to cliffs,
where sand martins nest; 01938 555654;
www.montwt.co.uk

- **Dolforwyn Castle, near Abermule:** partially
restored castle, built by the last Prince of
Gwynedd, Llewelyn ap Gruffydd, in 1277;
set on a wooded ridge overlooking the
Severn Valley; 01443 336000;
http://cadw.wales.gov.uk

TRAIN STATIONS
Newtown.

BIKE HIRE
None locally.
- **For spares, etc.: Sapphire Cycles, Newtown:**
01686 610021; www.sapphire-cycles.co.uk

FURTHER INFORMATION
- To view or print National Cycle Network
routes, visit www.sustrans.org.uk
- Maps for this area are available to buy from
www.sustransshop.co.uk
- For further information on routes in Wales,
visit www.routes2ride.org.uk/wales
- **Welshpool Tourist Information:** 01686
625580; http://tourism.powys.gov.uk
- **Wales Tourist Information:** 0870 830 0306;
www.visitwales.co.uk

ROUTE DESCRIPTION
The traffic-free riverside cyclepath follows the
south side of the River Severn, to pass
Newport's Tourist Information Centre. Follow
the Route 81 signs for Welshpool (Y Trallwng).

Montgomery Canal

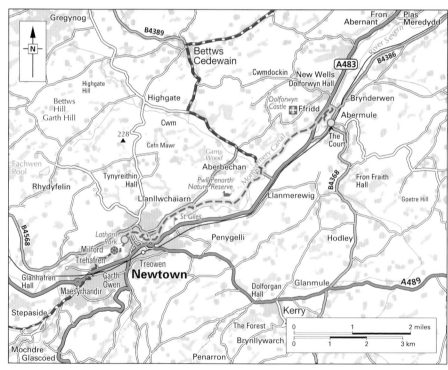

The route soon crosses the river, continuing on a traffic-free cyclepath, to run by the north bank and parallel to Canal Road. Soon join a new traffic-free section, which avoids the previously followed B4568. This pleasant stretch joins the Montgomery Canal Greenway and continues to Aberbechan, parting company with Route 81. From Aberbechan, the route continues for a further 2 miles (3km) to Abermule on a traffic-free cyclepath.

NEARBY CYCLE ROUTES

The Newtown to Abermule trail shares the first half of its length with National Route 81. Known as Lôn Cambria, this crosses the heart of mid-Wales between Aberystwyth and Shrewsbury. The 113-mile (182km) ride leads along a mixture of river valleys, trails, mountain roads and country lanes, with fine views.

To the south of Newtown, the Radnor Ring (Regional Route 25) is a waymarked circular 84-mile (135km) route, which follows quiet country roads through some of mid-Wales' most spectacular scenery.

For mountain bikers, there are exciting off-road alternatives that climb to almost 545m (1,790ft). Mid-Wales also has a number of Wales Cycle Breaks Centres at Rhayader, Knighton/Presteigne and Brecon. Visit www.cyclebreakswales.com or www.gwyliaubeiciocymru.com for details.

Swans and cygnets on the canal

MAWDDACH TRAIL

Starting right in the heart of the handsome grey stone town of Dolgellau, the Mawddach Trail/Lôn Mawddach runs alongside the estuary of Afon Mawddach, below the foothills of Cadair Idris, which rises to a height of over 892m (2,927ft), with views across to the hills in the north. There are two atmospheric wooden bridges on the trail: the toll bridge at Penmaenpool for road traffic and the bridge at the mouth of the estuary, which carries the railway line, pedestrians and cyclists into the seaside town of Barmouth. The area around the whole route is abundant in birdlife and, if you are lucky, you may even spot a seal. If you choose to go into the heart of Barmouth, with its sandy beaches and a wide choice of refreshments, you will need to cycle for about 0.75 miles (1.2km) on-road.

Dolgellau has become a cycling hub principally because of its proximity to the mountain bike trails in Coed y Brenin Forest, a few miles to the north, but also because of its location on Lôn Las Cymru (National Routes 8 and 82). On this trail, there are two options north to Porthmadog and two options south to Machynlleth.

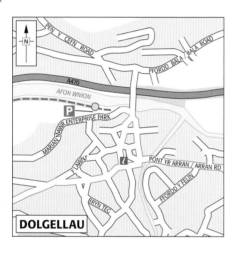

ROUTE INFORMATION
National Route: 8
Start: Main car park in Dolgellau.
Finish: Barmouth Promenade.
Distance: 10 miles (16km).
Grade: Easy.
Surface: Tarmac or gravel.
Hills: None.

YOUNG & INEXPERIENCED CYCLISTS
Traffic-free from Dolgellau as far as the wooden railway bridge near Barmouth, then on-road into town. Special care should be taken on the A496 on the approach to Barmouth.

REFRESHMENTS
• Lots of choice in Dolgellau.
• George III pub, Penmaenpool: on the water's edge with good food; very popular with cyclists.
• Lots of choice in Barmouth.

THINGS TO SEE & DO
• **Dolgellau:** a handsome town with 17th- and 18th-century grey stone buildings.
• **Cadair Idris:** 892m (2,927ft) high mountain.

Easy level cycling on the Mawddach Trail

Afon Mawddach Estuary

- **Arthog Bog:** wetland, with more than 130 species of plant; www.rspb.org.uk
- **Mawddach Estuary:** once a shipbuilding centre where, between 1770 and 1827, over 100 boats were made from the local oak to be found along the estuary.
- **Barmouth:** picturesque seaside resort.

TRAIN STATIONS
Morfa Mawddach; Barmouth.

BIKE HIRE
- Dolgellau Cycles, Dolgellau: 01341 423332; www.dolgellaucycles.co.uk

MAWDDACH TRAIL

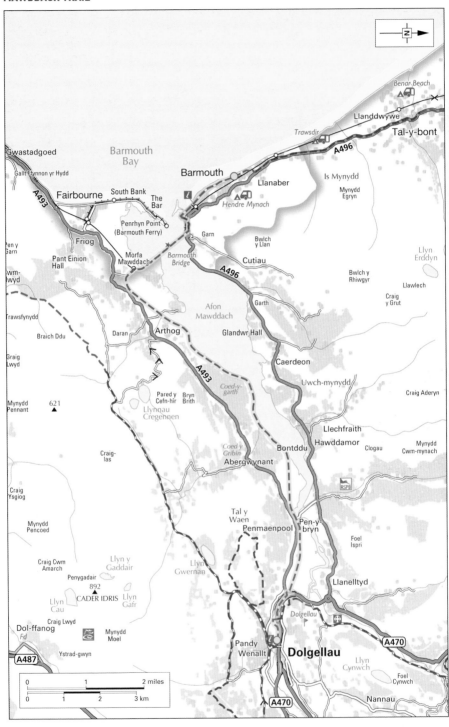

Precipice Walk, north of Dolgellau

FURTHER INFORMATION

- To view or print National Cycle Network routes, visit www.sustrans.org.uk
- Maps for this area are available to buy from www.sustransshop.co.uk
- For more information on routes in Wales, visit www.routes2ride.org.uk/wales
- Barmouth Tourist Information: 01341 280787; www.barmouth-wales.co.uk
- Dolgellau Tourist Information: 01341 422888
- Wales Tourist Information: 0870 830 0306; www.visitwales.co.uk

ROUTE DESCRIPTION

The trail starts in the heart of Dolgellau, from the corner of the main car park by the bridge over the River Wnion. It follows the river out of Dolgellau and continues along the south side of the Mawddach Estuary on the course of the old railway line from Barmouth to Ruabon – the line opened in 1869 to take Victorian holidaymakers to the fashionable resort of Barmouth. It closed in 1965. At the mouth of the estuary, use Barmouth Bridge to cross towards Barmouth. There is a short section on the A496 on the approach to the town where care is needed. Take Beach Road to the Promenade.

NEARBY CYCLE ROUTES

Lôn Mawddach is on National Route 8, which goes south to Cardiff via Machynlleth, Rhayader and Builth Wells, and north to Bangor.

There are lots of mountain bike trails in Coed y Brenin Forest, to the north of Dolgellau (see page 98). Lôn Las Cymru continues north via Coed y Brenin on Routes 8 and 82 to Holyhead.

SNOWDON EXPERIENCE – COED Y BRENIN TO GELLILYDAN, VIA TRAWSFYNYDD

Coed y Brenin is where mountain biking began in Wales, and it remains one of the favourite destinations for bikers. There are more than 60 miles (97km) of trails to explore, with something for everyone, from novices to the national champions who still ride its more challenging trails.

Why not take a spin before you set off on this ride, part of the exciting National Route 82. This will take you through parts of Snowdonia National Park that few see, and offers a satisfying ride in the saddle, although there are a few hills. The final section from Trawsfynydd to Gellilydan is much easier and makes for a great family ride. It passes the reservoir of Llyn Trawsfynydd, the third largest body of water in Wales, constructed in the 1920s to supply cooling water to the Trawsfynydd nuclear power station. From its shores, there are superb views of the Rhinogs and Cadair Idris.

Some 80 per cent of the inhabitants of Trawsfynydd have Welsh as their first language. The village is also the birthplace of St John Roberts, one of the Forty Martyrs of England and Wales, who helped plague sufferers in London. Unfortunately, he fell foul of King James I, was found guilty of high treason, and was hung, drawn and quartered in December 1610.

ROUTE INFORMATION
National Route: 82
Start: Coed y Brenin Visitor Centre.
Finish: Gellilydan.

Coed y Brenin Visitor Centre

Distance: 13 miles (21km).
Grade: Moderate to challenging. The final section from Trawsfynydd to Gellilydan is easy.
Surface: Tarmac, forest roads and gravel cyclepath.
Hills: Quite hilly, with three substantial climbs from the start point to Gilfach Wen. There is a last small climb into Trawsfynydd, then it's downhill to the finish.

YOUNG & INEXPERIENCED CYCLISTS
The final section from Trawsfynydd to Gellilydan is ideal for families, provided care is taken on the road sections. Coed y Brenin to Trawsfynydd is on quiet lanes and forest roads.

REFRESHMENTS
- Cafe in Coed y Brenin Visitor Centre.
- Various options in Trawsfynydd.
- Bryn Arms pub, Gellilydan.

THINGS TO SEE & DO
- Dolmelynllyn Estate, Ganllwyd, 2 miles south of start: includes the Coed Ganllwyd National

Cadair Idris

Nature Reserve and an old gold mine on the moorland of Cefn Coch; 01492 860123; www.nationaltrust.org.uk

- **Hermon Forest Car Park, near Ganllwyd, Coed y Brenin Forest**: deep in the woods, this is an ideal location from which to plan your own trips in the more remote areas of the Forest Park; for cyclists, there's open access on the forest roads, waymarked cycle routes and bridleways; www.forestry.gov.uk

- **Trawsfynydd Power Station**: take a tour of this decommissioned nuclear power station on the shores of pretty Llyn Trawsfynydd; 01766 540622

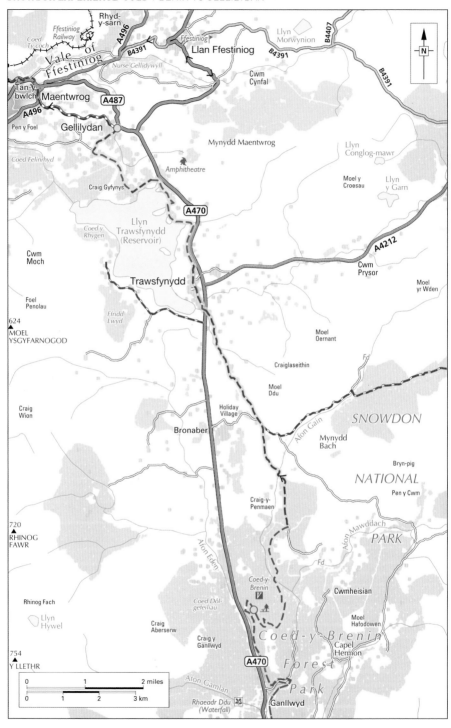

Snow above Trawsfynydd

- **Ffestiniog Railway, Porthmadog:** historic railway, which climbs spectacularly from the harbour in Porthmadog to the slate-quarrying town of Blaenau Ffestiniog; 01766 516024; www.festrail.co.uk

TRAIN STATIONS
None.

BIKE HIRE
- **Beics Brenin, at Coed y Brenin Visitor Centre:** 01341 440728; www.beicsbrenin.co.uk
- **Trawsfynydd Holiday Village Mountain Bike Hire, Bronaber, Trawsfynydd:** 01766 540219; www.logcabins-skiwales.co.uk

FURTHER INFORMATION
- To view or print National Cycle Network routes, visit www.sustrans.org.uk
- Maps for this area are available to buy from www.sustransshop.co.uk
- For further information on routes in Wales, visit www.routes2ride.org.uk/wales
- Snowdonia Tourist Information: www.visitsnowdonia.info
- Wales Tourist Information: 0870 830 0306; www.visitwales.co.uk

ROUTE DESCRIPTION
This route is easily followed as National Route 82 passes right by the new, iconic, cone-roofed Coed y Brenin Visitor Centre. Follow the signs to work your way up north through the forest. After approximately 4 miles (6.5km), the route joins a very quiet minor road, which leads out from the trees and soon passes by Gilfach Wen.

Most of the climbing is over now, and the remainder of the route, from Trawsfynydd to Gellilydan, is easy cycling, following the east side of pretty Llyn Trawsfynydd.

NEARBY CYCLE ROUTES
This trail is part of the longer National Route 82. Combined with National Route 8, it forms Lôn Las Cymru, which extends for 251 miles (404km) from Holyhead to Cardiff or Chepstow. Lôn Las Cymru passes a variety of landscapes, from the rural lanes of Anglesey to the valleys of south Wales. It also cuts through the magnificent National Parks of Snowdonia and the Brecon Beacons.

Coed y Brenin is home to some of the finest mountain biking in the UK, with waymarked trails and a new family route, all starting from the new visitor centre at Dolgefeilliau. There's a great childrens' play area and a cafe with views to die for: www.forestry.gov.uk

LÔN EIFION & LÔN LAS MENAI

Caernarfon is dominated by the towers and battlements of its mighty castle, built for Edward I in the 13th century, to command the entrance to the Menai Strait. Its unique polygonal towers, intimidating battlements and colour-banded walls were designed to echo Constantinople, the imperial power of Rome and the dream castle of Welsh myth and legend. Inside the walled town, there are narrow streets lined with ancient houses, shops and inns. On the higher ground on the east side of the town is the site of the old Roman fort of Segontium.

The investiture of Charles, the Prince of Wales, was held in the castle on 1 July 1969. Ironically, Caernarfon is a focus for the cause of Welsh nationalism and has the highest proportion (86 per cent) of Welsh speakers in all of Wales.

Two railway paths start near the castle in Caernarfon. The longer of the two, Lôn Eifion, climbs south to Bryncir, with views out over Caernarfon Bay and inland towards Snowdonia; the shorter Lôn Las Menai runs northeast along the coast, linking Caernarfon with the old slate harbour of Y Felinheli.

ROUTE INFORMATION
National Route: 8
Travelling south on Lôn Eifion:
Start: Caernarfon Castle.

Finish: Bryncir.
Travelling northeast on Lôn Las Menai:
Start: Victoria Dock, Caernarfon.
Finish: Garddfon Inn, Y Felinheli.

Distance: Lôn Eifion: 12.5 miles (20km). Lôn Las Menai: 4 miles (6.5km). **Grade:** Easy to moderate from Caernarfon to Bryncir; easy from Caernarfon to Y Felinheli. **Surface:** Tarmac. **Hills:** Lôn Eifion: long steady climb of 152m (499ft) over approximately 10 miles (16km) from Caernarfon to the radio mast, 2 miles (3km) south of Penygroes. **Lôn Menai:** no hills, although there is a short climb on the edge of Y Felinheli.

CAERNARFON

Victoria Dock

Caernarfon Castle

Caernarfon Castle, floodlit by night

YOUNG & INEXPERIENCED CYCLISTS

Lôn Eifion: All traffic-free but there are short road sections to leave the centre of Caernarfon.
Lôn Las Menai: Traffic-free but there are short road sections to navigate the centres of Caernarfon and Y Felinheli.

REFRESHMENTS

- Lots of choice in Caernarfon.
- Pubs and small shops in communities along the route.
- Cafe at Inigo Jones Slate Works, Groeslon.
- Pubs and cafes in Penygroes.
- Pub and a garden centre cafe in Bryncir.
- Pubs and small shops in Y Felinheli.

THINGS TO SEE & DO

- **Caernarfon Castle:** medieval castle; 01286 677617; http://cadw.wales.gov.uk
- **Welsh Highland Railway:** mountain railway line, which closed in the 1930s and is now being reopened, with the section from Caernarfon to Hafod y Llyn already open; 01286 677018; www.festrail.co.uk
- **Dramatic views of Snowdonia.**
- Inigo Jones Slate Works, Groeslon: workshops and showrooms, where you can see craftsmen cut, shape and polish raw slate slabs into practical products such as kitchen worktops and different craft items; 01286 830242; www.inigojones.co.uk
- **Menai Strait:** channel separating the island of Anglesey from the mainland.
- **Menai Suspension Bridge:** opened in 1826, this bridge over the Menai Strait was designed by Thomas Telford to help reduce the travel time from London to Holyhead; www.anglesey-history.co.uk
- **Britannia Bridge:** rail bridge across the Menai Strait designed by Robert Stephenson, son of the locomotive pioneer George Stephenson; www.anglesey-history.co.uk
- **Superb views of the island of Anglesey.**

TRAIN STATIONS

Bangor. Narrow-gauge steam railway stations at Caernarfon, Bontnewydd and Dinas.

BIKE HIRE

- **Beics Menai Cycles, Caernarfon:** 01286 676804; www.beicsmenai.co.uk

FURTHER INFORMATION

- To view or print National Cycle Network routes, visit www.sustrans.org.uk
- Maps for this area are available to buy from www.sustransshop.co.uk

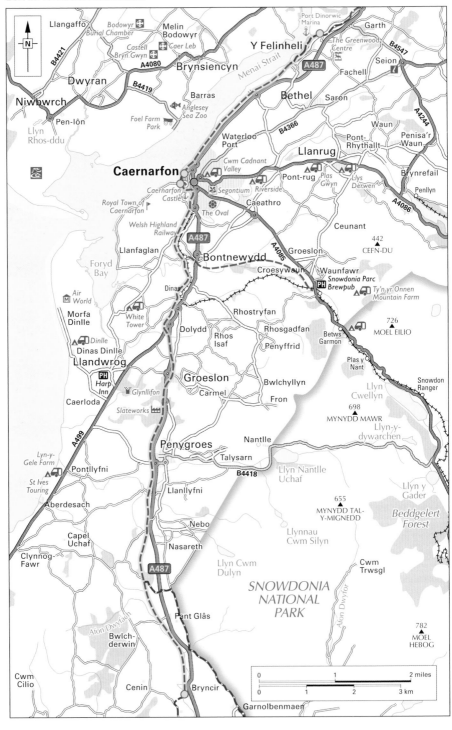

- Caernarfon Tourist Information: 01286 672232; www.visitcaernarfon.com
- Wales Tourist Information: 0870 830 0306; www.visitwales.co.uk

ROUTE DESCRIPTION

Lôn Eifion: Join National Route 8 as it passes between the castle and the town square and then turns south into St Helen's Road, passing the dock buildings. After 364m (400 yards), you will see the Welsh Highland Railway, and immediately after the station turn left onto the Lôn Eifion cyclepath. As you ride along the path, don't be surprised to see a steam locomotive alongside you.

Pass under the Lôn Eifion signs to climb gradually through delightful woods. After 2 miles (3km), approach the station at Dinas. Here, the railway peels off east, while the cycle route continues south. In another couple of miles, pass the Inigo Jones Slate Works.

You soon reach the village of Penygroes, 7 miles (11km) from Caernarfon. Lôn Eifion climbs into wilder scenery, with excellent views of Snowdonia and the hills of the Lleyn Peninsula. After 9 miles (14.5km) you reach the highest point, close to some gravel pits. Now you can enjoy a gentle downhill stretch until the cycleway ends at the village of Bryncir. Route 8 joins a minor road and turns right. However, at this point, you can also turn left into Bryncir.

To extend the ride, press on to Criccieth. Although the route is mainly on-road from Bryncir, it's a very enjoyable ride on country lanes and through villages. After turning right, follow the signs for Route 8 through a farmyard and then on quiet lanes to the village of Llanystumdwy, which was home to the famous Welsh politician David Lloyd George. The route crosses over the bridge and turns left, passing the Lloyd George Memorial. From here, it is just a couple of miles to the pretty seaside town of Criccieth, with its excellent views over Cardigan Bay.

Cycling through the Lôn Eifion gateway

Lôn Las Menai: From Victoria Dock in Caernarfon, follow the 4-mile (6.5km) railway path through broadleaf woodland to the old slate harbour of Y Felinheli (Port Dinorwig). There are views of the Menai Strait and across the water to the island of Anglesey. You'll also see two famous bridges: the Menai Suspension Bridge and the Britannia Bridge.

NEARBY CYCLE ROUTES

Lôn Eifion and Lôn Las Menai form part of National Route 8, Lôn Las Cymru, which links Holyhead to Cardiff. Regional Route 61 (Lôn Gwyrfai) joins Route 8 (Lôn Eifion) just south of Caernarfon and goes to Waunfawr.

National Route 5 follows the north Wales coast (see page 114). National Route 82 (Lôn Las Ogwen) runs south of Bangor (see page 110).

LÔN LAS CEFNI – NEWBOROUGH TO LLYN CEFNI

From the southwest corner of Anglesey to the reservoir of Llyn Cefni, enjoy some fine flat cycling on pretty country lanes and traffic-free cyclepaths. The views are extensive, and there's a satisfying feeling of progression as you pass through the various types of terrain.

Birdwatchers, in particular, will be in their element, as the route passes by several important wetland habitats. One of these is Malltraeth Sands, where the cyclepath follows a cob, or dyke, constructed in the 19th century, after several attempts, as a flood barrier. Some land was reclaimed on the inland side but there is still plenty of wildlife-rich marshland. This was a favourite area of Newborough-born Charles Tunnicliffe, internationally renowned as a wildlife painter.

From there, the route swings inland to follow the Cefni River on a long straight track – you could be forgiven for thinking you were in the Netherlands until you turn to look at the mountains on the mainland. The quiet market town of Llangefni is the largest settlement reached on the route. If time allows, make a detour to Oriel Ynys Môn (Anglesey Gallery). This attractive art gallery and museum lies on the edge of the small town. From Llangefni, it's a short pedal to the end of the route at Llyn Cefni, which is a perfect spot for a picnic.

ROUTE INFORMATION

National Route: Not a National Route, but links National Routes 5 and 8
Start: Northern edge of Newborough Forest.
Finish: Llyn Cefni.
Distance: 10 miles (16km).

Grade: Easy.
Surface: Tarmac and shale.
Hills: None.

YOUNG & INEXPERIENCED CYCLISTS

Ideal for novices and families with young

Low tide at Newborough Warren

The History Room at Oriel Ynys Môn

children, provided care is taken on the very quiet road sections and occasional road crossings.

REFRESHMENTS
- Various options in Newborough and Malltraeth.
- Lots of choice in Llangefni.

THINGS TO SEE & DO
- **Anglesey Model Village & Gardens, Parc Newborough, Llanfairpwllgwyngyll:** Anglesey landmarks shrunk to a scale of one-twelfth; also a model railway, which circles the gardens, stopping only at the world-famous station of Llanfairpwllgwyngyllgogerychwyrndrobwllllantysiliogogogoch, the longest town name in the world; 01248 440477; www.angleseymodelvillage.co.uk
- **Anglesey Bird World, Dwyran:** bird park and sanctuary, with more than 300 species and walk-through aviaries; 01248 440872; www.anglesey-bird-world.wales.info
- **Henblas Country Park, Bodorgan:** working farm with sheep-shearing and sheepdog

demonstrations, as well as the opportunity to help feed lambs at Easter; 01407 840440; www.parc-henblas-park.co.uk
- **Oriel Ynys Môn (Anglesey Gallery), Rhosmeirch, Llangefni:** showplace for local artists and craftspeople; includes fascinating exhibits illustrating the island's history, culture and wildlife; 01248 724444; www.croesomon.co.uk

TRAIN STATIONS
Bodorgan.

BIKE HIRE
- **Isle of Anglesey Bike and Kayak Hire:** www.bikeandkayak.co.uk

FURTHER INFORMATION
- To view or print National Cycle Network routes, visit www.sustrans.org.uk
- Maps for this area are available to buy from www.sustransshop.co.uk
- For further information on routes in Wales, visit www.routes2ride.org.uk/wales

LLANGEFNI

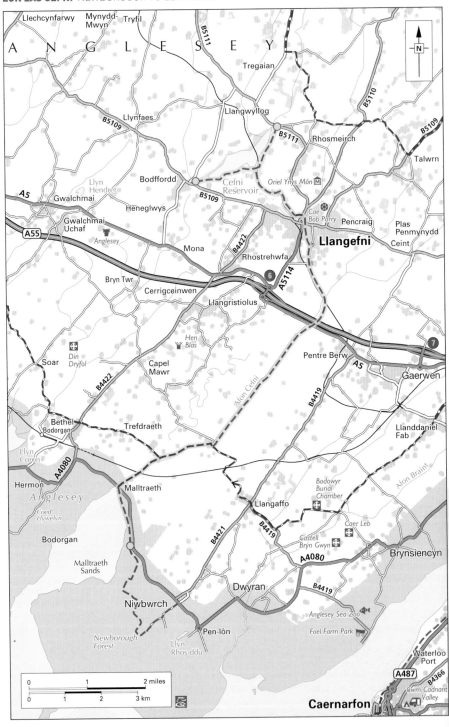

One of the artworks along the route

LÔN LAS CEFNI NEWBOROUGH TO LLYN CEFNI

giant seed pods and split oak timbers revealing the poem 'Nant y Pandy', by local poet Rolant o Fôn. Cycle alongside a disused railway line that follows the River Cefni up to Llyn Cefni, where you can enjoy a break overlooking the reservoir.

NEARBY CYCLE ROUTES

The Lôn Las Cefni cycleway is not part of the National Cycle Network. However, this excellent, mainly traffic-free trail can be followed to link with National Routes 5 and 8.

Route 5, the North Wales Coast Cycle Route, stretches for 105 miles (169km) from Holyhead to Chester. On Anglesey, it follows quiet lanes, linking with Route 8 by the town of Valley in the northwest, and has fine views across the Menai Strait to Snowdonia.

From Holyhead, Route 8 passes through Valley, following quiet minor roads around the southern half of Anglesey. After crossing the Menai Strait, the route (part of Lôn Las Cymru North) runs down through north Wales and Snowdonia National Park.

There is a network of traffic-free routes in Newborough Forest, from where you can extend your ride by following the Lôn Las Cefni signs all the way to the village of Newborough.

- **Anglesey Tourist Information:** 01248 750057; www.visitanglesey.co.uk
- **Wales Tourist Information:** 0870 830 0306; www.visitwales.co.uk

ROUTE DESCRIPTION

From Newborough Forest's northeast corner, cross the Malltraeth Cob with an estuary on your left and the Malltraeth Marsh to your right. Watch out for wildlife as you cross the marsh, which is an SSSI and RSPB reserve. Follow the Lôn Las Cefni signs for a short section on-road before rejoining the traffic-free path at Pont Marquis (Marquis Bridge). Follow the River Cefni to Llangefni (take care crossing the A5).

The route is signed through the centre of Llangefni and this is the best opportunity to take a break. Continue north from the town through The Dingle Local Nature Reserve, passing artworks such as a huge dragonfly,

Fishing boats in Cefni Reservoir

LÔN LAS OGWEN – BANGOR TO LLYN OGWEN

Arguably one of the most beautiful cycle rides in the entire country, this will take you deep into the embrace of the hills. Along the way you'll pass pretty woodlands, meadows, rivers and waterfalls. Naturally, as this is a route into the mountains, there's some uphill cycling, but we'll ignore that for now.

Lôn Las Ogwen owes its existence to slate quarrying. The ride starts by the Hirael Bay car park – the prized roofing material was exported worldwide from the quayside – and then follows the trackbed of the railway, which carried the slate down from the mountains. It's a delightful cycle, passing broadleaf woodland, the bubbling Afon Cegin and, in spring, a colourful array of primroses and other forest flowers.

Tregarth, and a welcoming pub, are soon reached. Don't be tempted to fill your glass too much, though, as the ride is just beginning. Continuing south, there are magnificent views of Snowdonia, but there is a price to pay for such pleasures – a 213m (699ft) ascent through the spoils of the slate quarries where waterfalls crash. This is Penrhyn Quarry, said to be the world's largest. Quarrying operations began back in 1770 under the slave-owning, anti-abolitionist MP Richard Pennant, who became the 1st Baron Penrhyn.

The journey ends at Ogwen Cottage at the head of Llyn Ogwen, a sparkling jewel beneath the splendid peaks of the Glyders. Rest and relax before a fun-filled return to the sea. You'll have earned it!

ROUTE INFORMATION
National Routes: 5, 82
Start: Hirael Bay car park, Bangor.
Finish: Ogwen Cottage, Llyn Ogwen.

Distance: 11 miles (17.5km). Shorter option: Bangor to Tregarth 4 miles (6.5km).
Grade: Bangor to Tregarth is easy/moderate; the rest of the route is challenging.
Surface: Tarmac and gravel.
Hills: The first 4 miles (6.5km) to Tregarth involve a gentle climb of less than 100m (328ft). Thereafter, there is a sustained, steep climb,

Primroses flourish along the route

BANGOR

110

Sheep and drystone walls enhance the route

with a further 300-odd metres (1,000ft) of ascent to Llyn Ogwen.

YOUNG & INEXPERIENCED CYCLISTS

The gentler, traffic-free section from Port Penrhyn (Bangor) to Tregarth is suitable for cycle-hardened children and novices. Beyond Tregarth the route is suitable only for fit and experienced cyclists.

REFRESHMENTS

- Lots of choice in Bangor.
- Pant Yr Ardd pub, Tregarth.
- Lakeside cafe at Llyn Ogwen.

THINGS TO SEE & DO

- **Penrhyn Castle, Bangor:** 19th-century fantasy castle, with a unique furniture collection, large gardens and grounds, and a formal Victorian walled garden; 01248 363219; www.nationaltrust.org.uk
- **Bangor Cathedral:** founded in about AD525, this low cathedral predates Canterbury by seven decades; dedicated to its founder, St Deiniol; www.churchinwales.org.uk
- **Gwynedd Museum & Art Gallery, Bangor:** boasting a collection that was begun in 1884 by Bangor University; remarkable museum covering archaeology, coins and medals, fine art and social history; 01248 353368; www.gwynedd.gov.uk/museums
- **Snowdonia National Park:** the ride passes into this magnificent national park, offering views of Snowdon, the highest peak in Wales and England, and beautiful Llyn Ogwen; 01248 352786; www.visitsnowdonia.info

Llyn Ogwen

TRAIN STATIONS
Bangor (Gwynedd).

BIKE HIRE
• Beics Menai Cycles, Caernarfon:
  01286 676804; www.beicsmenai.co.uk

FURTHER INFORMATION
• To view or print National Cycle Network
  routes, visit www.sustrans.org.uk
• Maps for this area are available to buy from
  www.sustransshop.co.uk
• For further information on routes in Wales,
  visit www.routes2ride.org.uk/wales
• Bangor Tourist Information: 01248 352786;
  www.visitsnowdonia.info
• Wales Tourist Information: 0870 830 0306;
  www.visitwales.co.uk

ROUTE DESCRIPTION
From the Hirael Bay car park in Bangor,
follow Route 5 to the east (signed Colwyn Bay)
along a traffic-free cyclepath. Further on, once
you've left the houses behind, join Route 82.
This traffic-free path leads pleasantly up the
valley of Afon Cegin to Tregarth, where there
is a pub.

From here, the route changes character as
it starts the steep climb through the spoils of a
slate quarry, on well-built stone paths
alongside the river to Llyn Ogwen. Route 82
continues on a section of the B4409, then a
traffic-free cyclepath, before tackling the
Ogwen Valley on a testingly steep minor
road, which ends at the foot of attractive
Llyn Ogwen.

No one should undertake the 305m (1,000ft)
climb to Llyn Ogwen unless they are in strong
physical shape.

NEARBY CYCLE ROUTES
Lôn Las Ogwen (Route 82) shares its start
point in Bangor with Route 5 and Route 8.
Route 5 is a popular traffic-free route that
leads across the border to Chester. It offers
a fabulous way to see this attractive stretch of
the north Wales coast. Lôn Las Cymru (Route 8)
is a long-distance route that passes through
the National Parks of the Brecon Beacons and
Snowdonia to the quiet lanes of Anglesey. This
challenging route incorporates the traffic-free
Lôn Eifion path to take you into the historic
town of Caernarfon (see page 102).

The intention is for Route 82 to continue as
an exciting loop through Snowdonia National
Park, passing through Betws-y-Coed and,
ultimately, allowing a fine circuit to be made to
Porthmadog (which is passed on Route 8).

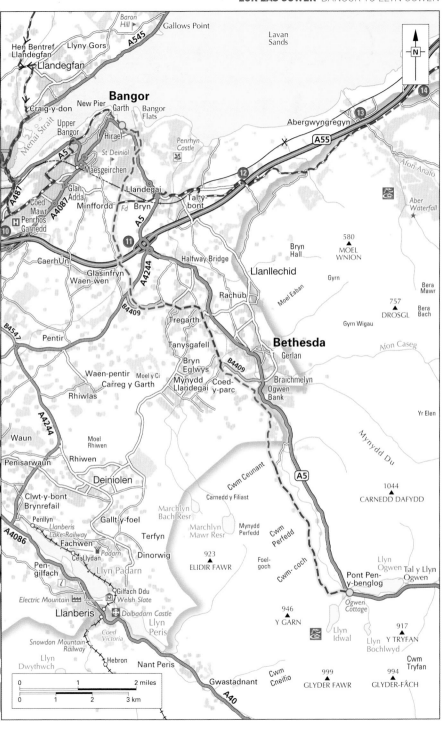

NORTH WALES COAST ROUTE – PRESTATYN TO RHOS-ON-SEA

Who doesn't love to cycle by the seaside? And when the route is flat, pleasant, traffic-free, full of glorious views and packed with things to do along the way – like this superb section of National Route 5 – it's perfect. For kids, especially, this route will appeal: there are numerous child-friendly attractions in the seaside towns and more than a few opportunities to grab an ice cream.

This part of the north Wales coast has hotter, sunnier summers than most – choose a breeze-free sunny day, if you can, and you'll have a ball. Magnificent sandy expanses flank most of the route, such as the beautiful beach at Colwyn Bay. This extends to the end of the cycle ride at Rhos-on-Sea, where you could always have a swim to cool off before enjoying fish and chips.

Rhos-on-Sea (Llandrillo-yn-Rhos), shortened to Rhos or Llandrillo, is named after the Welsh kingdom of Rhos established there in late Roman times as a sub-kingdom of Gwynedd. According to legend, Madog ap Owain Gwynedd, a Welsh prince of Gwynedd, sailed from here in 1170 and discovered America, more than 300 years before Christopher Columbus's famous voyage in 1492. Whether it's true or not, you might ask why he'd want to leave such a beautiful coastline in the first place.

ROUTE INFORMATION
National Route: 5
Start: Nova Centre, Prestatyn.
Finish: Rhos-on-Sea.
Distance: 16 miles (25.5km).
Grade: Easy.
Surface: Tarmac.
Hills: None, except for short climbs over the jetties at Llanddulas.

YOUNG & INEXPERIENCED CYCLISTS
An ideal route for novices and families with young children, as it's all traffic-free, apart from a very short section on the approach to Kinmel Bay.

REFRESHMENTS
• Lots of choice in Prestatyn, Rhyl, Pensarn, Colwyn Bay and Rhos-on-Sea.

THINGS TO SEE & DO
• SeaQuarium, Rhyl: see more than 50 native species of marine life and the dramatic Ocean Falls Cascade; follow an underwater

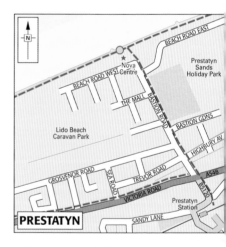

tunnel surrounded by sharks, rays and other fascinating creatures;
01745 344660; www.seaquarium.co.uk
• Sun Centre, Rhyl and Sky Tower, Rhyl Promenade: children will love the centre's water slides, set in a mock-tropical environment; rising above the centre is a 73m (240ft) rotating observation tower,

which gives superb views of the coast and Snowdonia; 01745 344433; www.rhylsuncentre.co.uk

- **The Holy Well & Chapel of St Trillo, Rhos-on-Sea:** minute church (it only holds some six worshippers), believed to date back to St Trillo, a 6th-century saint who established his 'Llan', an enclosure of land, in the area; 01492 530478; www.rhyl-prestatyn.co.uk

TRAIN STATIONS

Prestatyn; Rhyl; Abergele & Pensarn; Colwyn Bay.

BIKE HIRE

Enquire locally.

FURTHER INFORMATION

- To view or print National Cycle Network routes, visit www.sustrans.org.uk
- Maps for this area are available to buy from www.sustransshop.co.uk
- For further information on routes in Wales, visit www.routes2ride.org.uk/wales
- **Colwyn Bay Tourist Information:** 01492 530478; www.rhyl-prestatyn.co.uk
- **Wales Tourist Information:** 0870 830 0306; www.visitwales.co.uk

Seafront track in Prestatyn

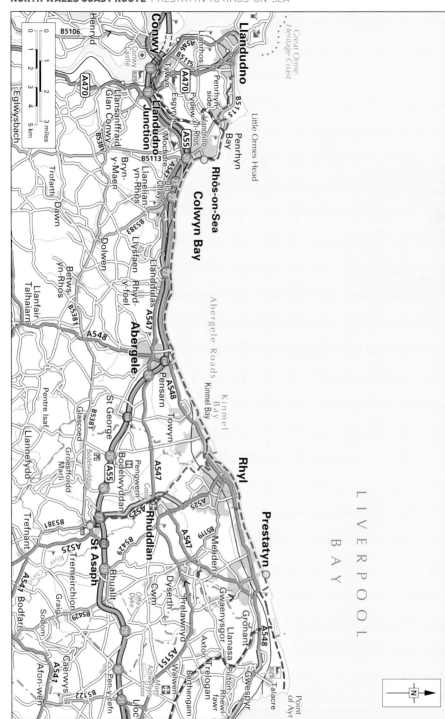

Marooned boats at
Rhos-on-Sea

ROUTE DESCRIPTION

One of the great advantages of cycling by the
sea is that route-finding is never much of a
problem. You'll be pleased that this seaside
route is no exception!

From the Nova Centre, Prestatyn, simply
follow the Route 5 signs west, towards Colwyn
Bay, along the seaside promenade.

At present, the route is traffic-free, apart
from a short section that includes the bridge
over the River Clwyd between Rhyl and Kinmel
Bay. However, following the success of a
Connect2 Big Lottery Fund bid, a new Foryd
Harbour bridge is to be constructed, which will
link the West Parade at Rhyl and Foryd
Harbour, and also connect to the existing
coastal path west of Rhyl.

Cycle on past Colwyn Bay to the finish point
at Rhos-on-Sea.

Note that, depending on the wind direction
on the day – it generally prevails from the west
– you may wish to ride this route in reverse.

NEARBY CYCLE ROUTES

The Prestatyn to Rhos-on-Sea trail is part of
the longer North Wales Coast Cycle Route
(National Route 5). This stretches for 105 miles
(169km) from Holyhead to Chester, passing

Cycling past sea
defences at Colwyn Bay

through the seaside towns of Llandudno,
Colwyn Bay, Rhyl and Prestatyn (there is a
newly opened, traffic-free section to the east
of Prestatyn). The majority of the route is
traffic-free and ideal for short day rides, with
the option of catching a train back to the start.

Route 84 links St Asaph with Route 5 to the
west of Rhyl, following the River Clwyd to
Rhuddlan (see page 118). It is all traffic-free,
with the exception of a short section to the
south of Rhuddlan.

There are also local routes which can be
followed from St Asaph for short circular rides,
as well as longer routes that extend south of
the town up the Vale of Clwyd.

LÔN CLWYD – ST ASAPH TO RHYL

The attractive historical city of St Asaph marks the start of this easy ride to the north Wales coast. It's worth spending some time exploring the old city before you head off.

St Asaph is reputed to have the smallest ancient cathedral in Britain. This diminutive place of worship belies its contribution to the Welsh nation – it was here that Bishop Morgan translated the Bible into Welsh (it was published in 1588). This was an act of great significance for the history and continuing survival of the language. The present building, which features many Victorian alterations, was begun in the 13th century on the site of a church established by St Asaph's predecessor, St Kentigern, in AD560.

Cycle on, easily, to Rhuddlan, where you are met by another historical landmark – Rhuddlan Castle. This dates from 1277 and was the second of the great Welsh fortifications built by the English monarch Edward I as part of his ambitious plan to conquer all of Britain. The strikingly symmetrical castle is dominated by a distinctive diamond-shaped inner ward. Outside, the River Clwyd was canalized and defended by a watergate and dock, and the four-storey Gillot's Tower overlooked it all. Not a place to attack lightly! The sea and Rhyl are soon reached on a lovely level cyclepath.

Rhuddlan Castle

LÔN CLWYD ST ASAPH TO RHYL

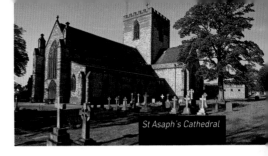
St Asaph's Cathedral

ROUTE INFORMATION
National Routes: 84, 5
Start: The Roe, St Asaph.
Finish: SeaQuarium, Rhyl Promenade.
Distance: 7 miles (11km).
Grade: Easy.
Surface: Tarmac.
Hills: None.

YOUNG & INEXPERIENCED CYCLISTS
An ideal route for novices and families with young
children, as it's all traffic-free, apart from a very
short section in St Asaph (which can be walked),
on the approach to Rhuddlan, and an on-road

section in Rhyl where you cross the railway and
young children should be supervised.

REFRESHMENTS
• Lots of choice in St Asaph, Rhuddlan and Rhyl.

THINGS TO SEE & DO
• St Asaph's Cathedral: 01745 582245;
  www.churchinwales.org.uk

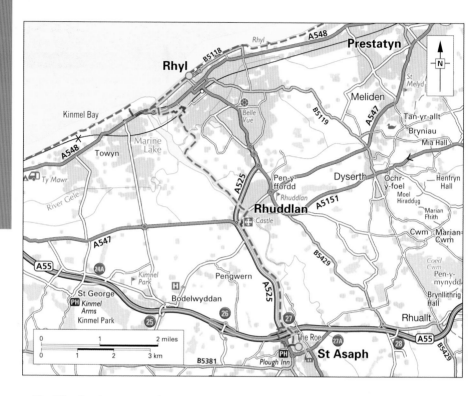

- Rhuddlan Castle: one of the 'iron ring' of fortresses built by the English monarch Edward I in his 13th-century campaign to conquer all of Britain; 01745 590777; www.rhyl.com
- SeaQuarium, Rhyl: see more than 50 native species of marine life and the dramatic Ocean Falls Cascade; follow an underwater tunnel surrounded by sharks, rays and other fascinating creatures; 01745 344660; www.seaquarium.co.uk
- Sun Centre, Rhyl and Sky Tower, Rhyl Promenade: children will love the centre's water slides, set in a mock-tropical environment; rising above the centre is a 73m (240ft) rotating observation tower, which gives superb views of the coast and Snowdonia; 01745 344433; www.rhylsuncentre.co.uk

- Roman Bath House, near Prestatyn: well-preserved remains, built in about AD 120 and extended about 30 years later; www.chesterwalls.infobaths.html

TRAIN STATIONS
Rhyl.

BIKE HIRE
Enquire locally.

FURTHER INFORMATION
- To view or print National Cycle Network routes, visit www.sustrans.org.uk
- Maps for this area are available to buy from www.sustransshop.co.uk
- For further information on routes in Wales, visit www.routes2ride.org.uk/wales
- Rhyl Tourist Information: 01745 344515;

Station for the prom railway at Rhyl

www.rhyl-prestatyn.co.uk
- **Wales Tourist Information:** 0870 830 0306; www.visitwales.co.uk

ROUTE DESCRIPTION

This is quite an easy route to follow and should be well signed throughout. From the lower part of the historical city of St Asaph, follow Route 84 signs to cross the River Elwy on a bridge that leads to a newly built section of riverside path. Further on, this joins an older section of traffic-free cyclepath, which runs parallel to the A525. There's a short on-road section as you come into Rhuddlan, with castle views.

Route 84 continues as a pleasant traffic-free cyclepath by the east bank of the River Clwyd. Further on, there is a link to the Brickfields Pond Nature Reserve. There is a short on-road section where you cross the railway and young children may need supervision. Route 84 joins Route 5, where the river meets the sea, and you can pedal the promenade cyclepath to Rhyl.

NEARBY CYCLE ROUTES

The end of this route shares the coastal section with the North Wales Coast Cycle Route (National Route 5), stretching for 105 miles (169km) from Holyhead to Chester, passing through the seaside towns of Llandudno, Colwyn Bay, Rhyl and Prestatyn (there is a new traffic-free section to the east of Prestatyn). The majority of the route is traffic-free and ideal for day rides, with the option of catching a train back to the start (see page 114).

There are also local routes which can be followed from St Asaph for short circular rides, as well as longer routes that extend to the south of the town up the Vale of Clwyd.

A BORDER FORAY – CONNAH'S QUAY TO CHESTER

Take a trip back in time, on a traffic-free old railway path, to the ancient city of Chester. The English border city never fails to impress with its unique atmosphere. The historic centre flourished as a port until the silting of the River Dee in the 15th century. Today it is still ringed by medieval walls, with fragments dating back to Saxon and even Roman times, and it is the only town in England to have preserved its walls in their entirety. These offer a 2-mile (3km) perimeter walk, with fine views of the city and the surrounding countryside. And, on the south side of the city centre, you can visit the site of a Roman amphitheatre.

From Hawarden Bridge, by Connah's Quay, the route is all traffic-free as it follows the former Mickle Trafford to Dee Marsh freight railway line – this once carried steel to and from the steelworks on the banks of the Dee at Hawarden Bridge. The attractive open ride, part of National Route 5, leads out into the surrounding fertile farmland, planted with potatoes, maize and grain. Near Chester, the railway path intersects with the towpath of the Shropshire Union Canal, which provides an excellent link to the centre of town.

ROUTE INFORMATION
National Route: 5
Start: Dock Road car park, Connah's Quay.

Finish: Shropshire Union Canal basin, off South View Road.
Distance: 8 miles (13km).

Grade: Easy.
Surface: Tarmac.
Hills: None.

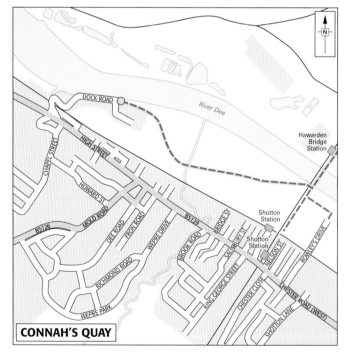

YOUNG & INEXPERIENCED CYCLISTS
Suitable for novices and families with young children.

REFRESHMENTS
• Lots of choice in Connah's Quay and Chester.

THINGS TO SEE & DO
• **Chester Cathedral:** dating from the 13th century, although legend has it that there was a prehistoric Druid

temple on this site, followed by a Roman temple dedicated to Apollo; 01244 324756; www.chestercathedral.com
- **Grosvenor Museum:** Roman archaeological finds, as well as displays on local history; 01244 402033; www.grosvenormuseum.co.uk
- **Chester Castle (Agricola Tower and Castle Walls):** Norman motte and bailey fortress, founded by Hugh de Avranches, Earl of Chester, and a must-see for visitors to the city; www.english-heritage.org.uk
- **Roman amphitheatre:** the largest Roman amphitheatre in Britain, used for both entertainment and military training; www.english-heritage.org.uk

King Charles' Tower and city walls, Chester

TRAIN STATIONS
Shotton; Hawarden Bridge; Chester.

BIKE HIRE
None.

FURTHER INFORMATION
- To view or print National Cycle Network routes, visit www.sustrans.org.uk
- Maps for this area are available to buy from www.sustransshop.co.uk
- **Chester Tourist Information:** 0845 647 7868; www.visitchester.com

ROUTE DESCRIPTION
Follow Route 5 signs from Dock Road car park, Connah's Quay, to Hawarden Bridge. The route for cyclists (and walkers) crosses the Dee at Hawarden Bridge on a new cantilevered structure. From there, the route takes you effortlessly through rich farmland, with the Clwydian Hills as a stunning backdrop.

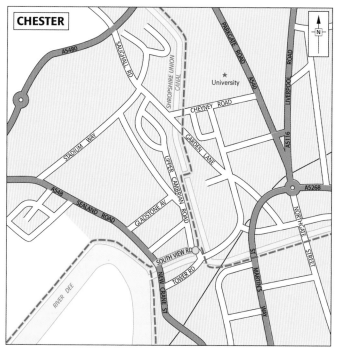

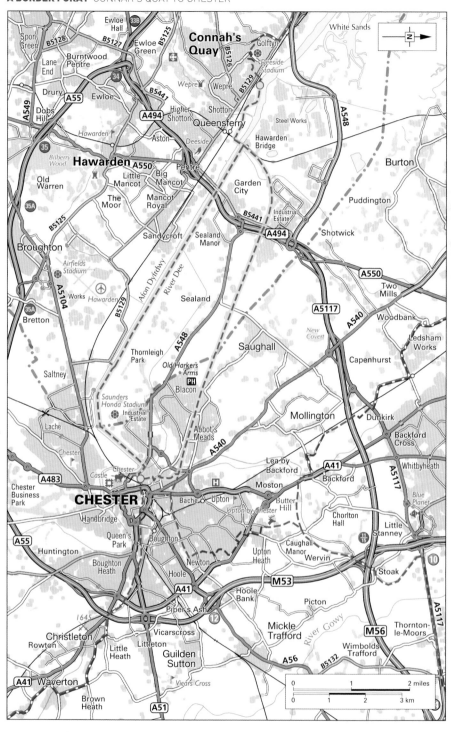

Boats on the Shropshire Union Canal

The Welsh/English border is crossed beyond Sealand, after which the route runs through Blacon. Further on, the railway path meets the Shropshire Union Canal towpath near the water meadow at Abbot's Meads. Follow the towpath, on the right, to reach the end of this route at the Shropshire Union Canal basin, just off South View Road. Chester train station can be easily reached by continuing along the canal towpath before following Egerton Street, Crewe Street and then City Road.

To return, you could catch a train back to Shotton station, by Connah's Quay, or pedal back on Regional Route 89 along an excellent trail on the north bank of the River Dee.

NEARBY CYCLE ROUTES

National Route 5 continues from Connah's Quay to the eastern outskirts of Flint, then resumes on-road to Prestatyn, where it continues traffic-free to the outskirts of Llandudno (see page 114). The railway path is being extended eastwards from Hoole to Mickle Trafford.

Other waymarked or traffic-free rides include: woodland paths in Delamere Forest Park, to the east of Chester; the Whitegate Way, a railway path lying just a little further east

Cycling over Hawarden Bridge

of Delamere; and a section of the Shropshire Union Canal between Chester and the waterways museum at Ellesmere Port.

NEXT STEPS...

We hope you have enjoyed the cycle rides in this book.

Sustrans developed the National Cycle Network to act as a catalyst for bringing cycling (and walking) back into our everyday lives. Between the 1950s and the mid-1970s cycling in the UK fell by 80%. Cycling now accounts for only about 2% of all journeys made in the UK, a fraction of what we used to achieve.

When you consider that nearly 6 in 10 car journeys are under 5 miles, it makes you wonder what the potential for increasing levels of cycling is. Evidence shows that, for local journeys under 5 miles, most of us could make 9 out of 10 journeys on foot, bike or public transport if there was more investment in making it possible to leave the car behind.

And why not? We can all be more savvy when it comes to travel. One small step becomes one giant leap if we all start walking away from less healthy lifestyles and pedalling our way towards happier children and a low carbon world.

And that's where Sustrans comes in. Sustainable travel means carbon-reducing, energy-efficient, calorie-burning, money-saving travel. Here are a few things that we think make sense. If you agree, join us.

- **Snail's pace** – 20mph or less on our streets where we live, go to school, shop and work – make it the norm, not just when there's snow or ice on the roads.

- **Closer encounters** – planning that focuses on good non-motorised access, so that we can reach more post offices, schools, shops, doctors and dentists without the car.

- **People spaces** – streets where kids can play hopscotch or football and be free-range, and where neighbours can meet and chat, and safe, local walking and cycling routes, to school and beyond.

- **Road revolution** – build miles and miles of bike paths that don't evaporate when they meet a road.

- **Find our feet** – campaign for pedestrian-friendly city centres, or wide boulevards with regular pedestrian crossings and slow-moving traffic.

- **Better buses** – used by millions, under-invested by billions and, if affordable, reliable and pleasant to use, could make local car journeys redundant.

- **More car clubs** – a car club on every street corner and several for every new-build estate.

- **Rewards for car-sharing** – get four in a car and take more than half the cars off the road.

- **Trains** – more of them, and cheaper.

- **Become a staycationer** – and holiday at home. Mountains, beaches, culture, great beer, good food and a National Cycle Network that connects them all.

If we work towards these goals we have a chance of delivering our fair share of the 80% reduction in CO_2 by mid-century that we're now committed to by law, and some of the 100% reduction that many climate experts now consider essential.

To find out more and join the movement, visit www.sustrans.org.uk

Free. Clean. Green.

Photo: Rita Platts/ Sustrans

Few people would say that they don't care about the environment, don't want to get fit or don't care about the damage pollution is doing to local communities – but what's the answer? The humble bike: a great way to get from A to B, cut carbon emissions and get fit at the same time. The bike is the greenest machine on the road, and Sustrans is doing everything it can to help people cycle more. Sustrans developed the National Cycle Network to help bring cycling (and walking) back into everyday life.

Cycling only accounts for 2% of all the journeys made in the UK today. 90% of all journeys under five miles could be made by foot, public transport or bike. And we are trying to do everything possible to make this happen. Help us provide everyone with a greener way to travel.

If you care about the environment and love cycling, you should support Sustrans. Get online at sustrans.org.uk, join the movement and find out how Sustrans can improve your cycling experience.

sustrans

JOIN THE MOVEMENT

ACKNOWLEDGEMENTS

Fergal MacErlean would like to thank the following for their assistance with writing this guide: Lee Waters, Ryland Jones, Gwyn Smith, Glyn Evans, Vinny Mott, Helen Davies and local Rangers.

The Automobile Association would like to thank the following photographers, companies and picture libraries for their assistance in the preparation of this book.

Abbreviations for the picture credits are as follows – (t) top; (b) bottom; (l) left; (r) right; (c) centre; (dps) double page spread; (AA) AA World Travel Library

Front cover: Harlech Castle with Snowdonia in the background; AA/M Bauer.
Back cover: Miranda Krestovnikoff; Sustrans.

3l Sustrans; 3r AA/S Watkins; 4 Sustrans; 5t AA; 5c Jon Bewley/Sustrans; 5b AA/D Croucher; 6/7 AA/M Bauer; 7tr Peter Knowles/Sustrans; 7cr David Angel/Alamy; 7br AA/I Burgum; 11tl Jon Bewley/Sustrans; 11tr Jon Bewley/Sustrans; 11c Jon Bewley/Sustrans; 11bc Andy Huntley/Sustrans; 11br Pru Comben/Sustrans; 13t Jon Bewley/Sustrans; 13c Nicola Jones/Sustrans; 13b Jon Bewley/Sustrans; 14 AA/R Duke; 15 AA/I Burgum; 17 AA/A J Hopkins; 18/19 AA/I Burgum; 19t Sustrans; 20 © Seb Rogers/Alamy; 21 Sustrans; 23 Sustrans; 25 © Richard Naude/Alamy; 26 AA/C Molyneux; 27 © The Photolibrary Wales/Alamy; 28c Julian Cram/Sustrans; 28b © Graham Morley/Alamy; 30b Jeff Morgan 12/Alamy; 31tr Chris Howes/Wild Places Photography/Alamy; 33tr CW Images/Alamy; 33b Sid Frisby/Alamy; 34 © The Photolibrary Wales/Alamy; 35 Sustrans; 37t © Kevin Round/Alamy; 37b © graham bell/Alamy; 38/39 © The Photolibrary Wales/Alamy; 40/41 © The Photolibrary Wales/Alamy; 41t Sustrans; 42/43 © The Photolibrary Wales/Alamy; 43t © Jeff Morgan heritage/Alamy; 45 © Rod McLean/Alamy; 46/47 AA/I Burgum; 49 © Matt Botwood

(CStock)/Alamy; 50/51 AA/M Moody; 51t © Bernard Castelein/naturepl.com; 53 © The Photolibrary Wales/Alamy; 54 AA; 55t © Seb Rogers/Alamy; 55b Jon Bewley/Sustrans; 57 © mkimages/Alamy; 58 AA/I Burgum; 59 AA/N Jenkins; 60/61 AA/C Jones; 61t Sustrans; 62/63 AA/I Burgum; 64 © Andrew Kneath/Alamy; 67 Peter Knowles/Sustrans; 69t Peter Knowles/Sustrans; 69c Peter Knowles/Sustrans; 70l © Mark Boulton/Alamy; 70r © The Photolibrary Wales/Alamy; 75t © greenwales/Alamy; 75b © Hugh Olliff/Alamy; 76/77 © Mark Boulton/Alamy; 77c AA/I Burgum; 78/79 AA/M Bauer; 79tr AA/N Jenkins; 80tl AA/M Bauer; 81b AA/M Bauer; 82 Glyn Evans/Sustrans; 83 AA/I Burgum; AA/A J Hopkins; 85 © Graham Eaton/naturepl.com; 86 AA/N Jenkins; 87t Julian Cram/Sustrans; 87b AA/N Jenkins; 89t Julian Cram/Sustrans; 89b AA/N Jenkins; 91l © powys photo/Alamy; 91r AA/C Molyneux; 92/93 © Jim Batty/Alamy; 93b AA/N Jenkins; 95t Julian Cram/Sustrans; AA/D Croucher; 95c AA/W Voysey; 97 AA/D Croucher; 98 © The Photolibrary Wales/Alamy; 99 AA/S Lewis; 101 © The Photolibrary Wales/Alamy; 103 AA/N Jenkins; 105 Sustrans; 106/107 © Camera Lucida/Alamy; 107t © The Photolibrary Wales/Alamy; 109t John Grimshaw/Sustrans; 109b © Ange/Alamy; 110 © Michael Hutchinson/naturepl.com; 111 Matt Davies/Sustrans; 112 © Paul Davies/Alamy; 115 © PBimages/Alamy; 117t © Chris Howes/Wild Places Photography/Alamy; 117c Dave Archer; 119t AA/C Molyneux; 118/119 AA/R Eames; 121 © Dave Ellison/Alamy; 123 AA/C Jones; 125t AA/A Tryner; 125b AA/T Marsh

Every effort has been made to trace the copyright holders, and we apologise in advance for any unintentional omissions or errors. We would be pleased to apply any corrections in the following edition of this publication.